IT'S A JUNGLE OUT THERE...

"I want a dog of which I can be proud," said Mrs. Kaliman. "Does that one have a good pedigree?"

"Lady," declared the kennel owner, "if he could talk, he wouldn't speak to either of us."

DOGGIE DANDIES! KITTY CACKLES! EVEN THE BIRDS AND THE BEES!

"What's smarter—a parrot or a chicken?"

"I don't know."

"Think about it—have you ever heard of Kentucky Fried Parrot?"

THE PERFECT BOOK FOR THE PET LOVER WHO HAS IT ALL... AND ALSO HAS TO CLEAN IT ALL UP!

THE ULTIMATE PET LOVER'S JOKE BOOK

BOOKS BY LARRY WILDE

The *Ultimate* Book of Ethnic Humor
The *Ultimate* Sex Maniacs Joke Book
The Official Computer Freaks Joke Book (with Steve Wozniak)
The Official Wasp Joke Book
The Official All America Joke Book
The *Ultimate* Lawyers Joke Book
The *Ultimate* Jewish Joke Book
More The Official Doctors Joke Book
The Official Executives Joke Book
The Official Sports Maniacs Joke Book
The *Absolutely Last* Official Sex Maniacs Joke Book
The Official Book of John Jokes
The Official Politicians Joke Book
The Official Rednecks Joke Book
The *Last* Official Smart Kids Joke Book
The *Absolutely Last* Official Polish Joke Book
The *Last* Official Irish Joke Book
The *Last* Official Sex Maniacs Joke Book
The Larry Wilde Book of Limericks
The Official Lawyers Joke Book
The Official Doctors Joke Book
More The Official Sex Maniacs Joke Book
The *Last* Official Jewish Joke Book

also

The Official Bedroom/Bathroom Joke Book
More The Official Smart Kids/Dumb Parents Joke Book
The Official Book of Sick Jokes
More The Official Jewish/Irish Joke Book
The *Last* Official Italian Joke Book
The Official Cat Lovers/Dog Lovers Joke Book
The Official Dirty Joke Book
The *Last* Official Polish Joke Book
The Official Golfers Joke Book
The Official Smart Kids/Dumb Parents Joke Book
The Official Religious/Not So Religious Joke Book
More The Official Polish/Italian Joke Book
The Official Black Folks/White Folks Joke Book
The Official Virgins/Sex Maniacs Joke Book
The Official Jewish/Irish Joke Book
The Official Polish/Italian Joke Book

and in hardcover

THE LARRY WILDE LIBRARY OF LAUGHTER
THE COMPLETE BOOK OF ETHNIC HUMOR
HOW THE GREAT COMEDY WRITERS CREATE
  LAUGHTER
THE GREAT COMEDIANS TALK ABOUT COMEDY

THE ULTIMATE PET LOVERS JOKE BOOK

by
Larry Wilde

BANTAM BOOKS
NEW YORK · TORONTO · LONDON · SYDNEY · AUCKLAND

THE ULTIMATE PET LOVERS JOKE BOOK

A Bantam Book / February 1990

Illustrations by Ron Wing.

ISBN 0-553-28343-X

Published simultaneously in the United States and Canada

Bantam Books are published by Bantam Books, a division of
Bantam Doubleday Dell Publishing Group, Inc. Its trademark,
consisting of the words ''Bantam Books'' and the portrayal of a
rooster, is Registered in U.S. Patent and Trademark Office and in
other countries. Marca Registrada. Bantam Books, 666 Fifth
Avenue, New York, New York 10103.

PRINTED IN THE UNITED STATES OF AMERICA

OPM   0 9 8 7 6 5 4 3 2 1

DEDICATION

Irwin Zucker
The Ultimate Pet
Lover

"I don't mind my children having pets until the pets start having children."

—Long Island Mother

Contents

Doggie Dandies

Fulton the animal lover was on his pet subject.

"There's no doubt that some dogs have almost human intelligence," he maintained.

"You may be right," agreed Palmer. "I often think that our Doberman tries to get on the good side of my wife by growling at me."

* * *

Sussman walked into a Manhattan pet shop.

"My wife wants to buy a little dog," said the New Yorker.

"What kind?" asked the owner.

"Any kind," replied Sussman, "so long as he wags his tail up and down."

"Why up and down?"

"We live in a tiny apartment. There isn't room for a dog that wags his tail sideways."

* * *

"I want a dog of which I can be proud," said Mrs. Kaliman. "Does that one have a good pedigree?"

"Lady," declared the kennel owner, "if he could talk, he wouldn't speak to either of us."

* * *

The Scotch terrier's leash was old and worn. During the night he broke it, got into the pantry, and ate all the food.

Next morning when Egerton heard the news from his wife, he asked, "Did the dog eat much?"

"He ate every single thing in the place," answered Mrs. Egerton, "except the dog biscuits."

* * *

Downey was dragged into court for keeping a dog without a license. Every time he tried to speak he was silenced by the court. Finally, the clerk demanded, "Is the court to understand you refuse to renew the license?"

"Yes, but—" began Downey.

"No buts," snapped the clerk. "You know your old license expired on June 30th?"

"I know," said Downey. "And so did the dog."

* * *

Did you hear about the army dog who wanted to be transferred to a new post?

* * *

Old Mrs. Callahan was walking her pet poodle at the end of a long leash. A big pack of stray dogs were following closely, sniffing away at the poodle.

A police officer approached the elderly woman and said, "Lady! Your dog's in heat!"

"Eat? She'll eat anything! Meat, fish, anything!"

"No," said the cop, "your dog should be *bred*!"

"Sure." Mrs. Callahan nodded. "White, rye, she'll eat anything!"

"Lady!" shouted the officer, "your dog should be *screwed*!"

"Go ahead! I always wanted a police dog!"

* * *

It was the first day of school and little Mikey was telling the teacher about his dog.

"And what kind of dog is it?" she inquired.

"Well, he's kind of mixed up," said the boy. "Sort of a cocker scandal."

* * *

Dave Millman, the San Jose computer advertising genius, gets guffaws with this gleeful gem:

Preston was having his hair cut in a barber shop. He noticed a dog sitting nearby watching the operation intently.

"I see your dog likes to watch you cut hair," said Preston.

"It ain't that," said the barber. "It's just that I sometimes snip off a bit of a customer's ear."

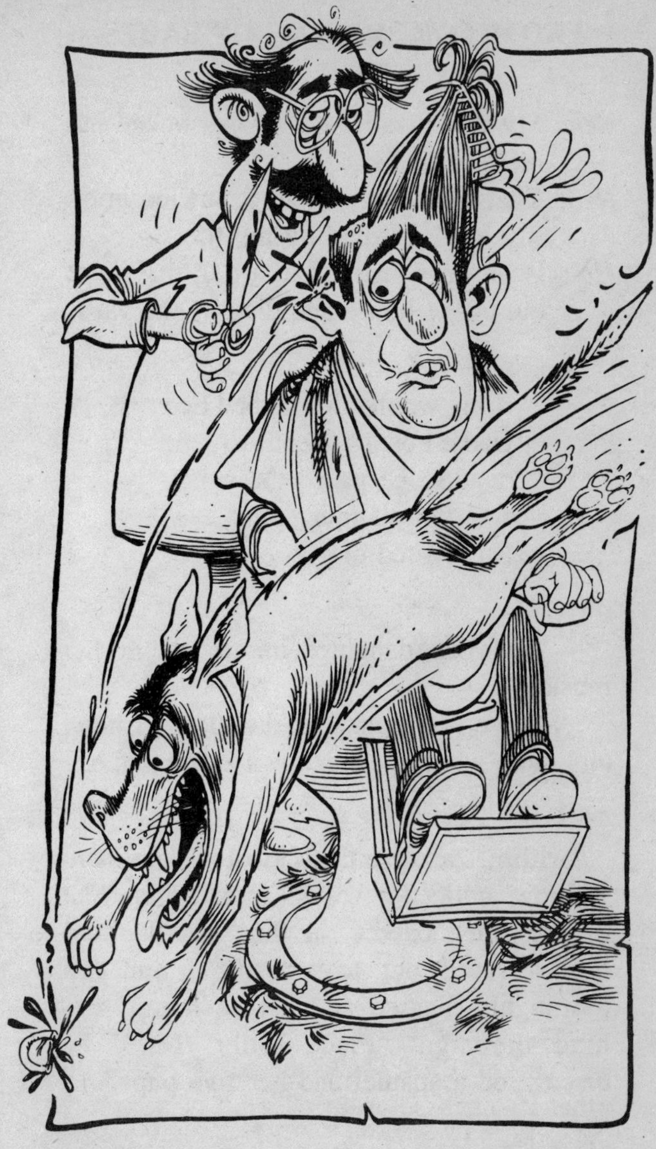

FROM THE MOUTHS OF BABES

Ken: My dog swallowed a tape worm and died by inches.

Neo: That's nothing, my dog crawled in on my bed and died by the foot.

Hal: I can beat that. I had a dog that went out of the house and died by the yard.

* * *

A big woolly dog named Lee
Had a host of friends to see.
So he paced the street
On all four feet
But visited mostly on three.

* * *

"Is your daughter improving in her music?"

"She certainly is. Our dog doesn't howl any more when she sits down at the piano."

* * *

Griffin, staring out his Boston apartment window, noticed a crowd gathered in front of the litter basket on the street corner. Griffin raced out to investigate and felt thoroughly pleased at what he found. Behind the sign "Place Litter Here" he discovered a spaniel and her five pups.

* * *

"This dog will eat off your hand."

"That's what I'm afraid of."

* * *

How are the bathrooms labeled at a dog show?

Pointers and Setters!

* * *

Farrell was training a greyhound in his backyard. When he thought the animal was ready for a trial he got a rabbit. Farrell then let the rabbit out on the road and sent the greyhound out after it. Ten minutes later his friend, Townsend, came by on a bicycle.

"Have you seen a rabbit and a dog out on the road?" asked Farrell.

"Yes," said Townsend. "The best race I've seen in years. When they passed me the dog was leading by five yards."

* * *

"I wanted to call my dog 'Shakespeare' but my mother wouldn't let me. She said it would be an insult to the man. Then I wanted to name him after you, but my mother wouldn't let me."

"Good for her."

"She said it would be an insult to the dog."

* * *

Fifi and Gigi, two French poodles, were visiting at a telephone pole. "Heard from your beau lately?" asked Fifi.

"Yes," replied Gigi. "I had a litter from him Friday."

* * *

Patricia Fripp, the magnificent speaker for all reasons, delights friends with this flash of frivolity:

"How much is that doggie in the window?"

"It's $50."

"And how much is the one in the shop? It looks like one from the same litter."

"Yes. That one is the twin. He's $55."

"Why the difference in price if they're identical puppies?"

"The one in the shop chewed up a $5 bill this morning."

* * *

Mrs. Van Cleve was giving a dinner party at her Long Island estate. Early in the evening Carlotta the cook said, "I don't like the way those mushrooms look. Maybe they're toadstools."

It was too late to send for other mushrooms, and Carlotta needed mushroom sauce for the entree.

"Try them on Ruffy," said Mrs. Van Cleve.

The dog ate them eagerly and begged for more. They decided to use the mushrooms.

The dinner was perfect. The guests enjoyed every course and were having coffee when Carlotta came in and whispered to Mrs. Van Cleve, "Ruffy is dead!"

The hostess excused herself and called up the hospital for an ambulance. Then she returned to her guests and tried to act cheerful. Soon she would see them froth at the mouth, scream, and drop dead. Wondering how she could tell when the symptoms began, Mrs. Van Cleve decided to look at Ruffy. She went into the kitchen and said to the cook, "Where is the dog? I want to see him."

"He's lying in the gutter," said Carlotta, "right where the car ran over him."

*　　*　　*

An explorer and his dog Duke were hopelessly lost far from civilization. After a few days, the man's hunger pangs became so great that he began to eye the animal. Finally, unable to stand it any longer, he built a fire, cooked the dog, and ate him. When he finished the meal, the explorer surveyed the pile of bones.

"Poor Duke," he sighed. "Oh, how he would've enjoyed those bones."

*　　*　　*

Barney Leason, the brilliant best-selling novelist, snatches smiles with this nutty nugget:

Mrs. Vanderslyke, the wealthy Mill Valley dowager, carried her Pekingese into a San Francisco department store. Thinking the dog might be thirsty, she let him slurp at the drinking fountain. An astonished security guard rushed over to her.

"Madam," he said, "I don't think our customers would like to drink out of that fountain after your dog."

"Oh, I beg your pardon," said the woman. "I thought it was for the clerks."

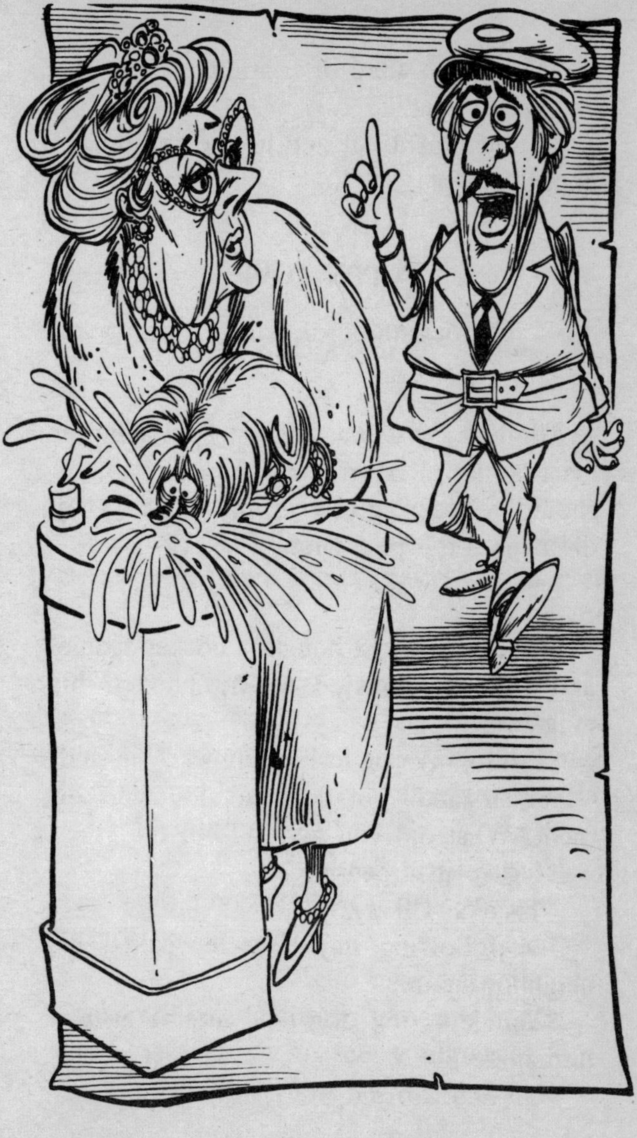

*   *   *

"My dog is hard of hearing."

"Why's that?"

"I told him to sit and he messed up the floor."

*   *   *

PUPPY LOVE

The beginning of a dog's life.

*   *   *

Admiral Byrd was showing an admirer his trophies. "By rights," he said, "these should've been given to my dogs. They discovered the pole first."

*   *   *

Wheeler had just bought a cocker spaniel and he was worried so he phoned his neighbor.

"I think my dog has distemper," he said. "I understand your dog had the same ailment. What did you give it?"

"I gave it turpentine."

"Thanks. I'll try it."

The following day Wheeler called his neighbor again.

"You jerk, my dog died after I gave it turpentine."

"Uh-huh. So did mine."

*   *   *

Dick was walking his dachshund and he met a friend who said, "What a funny-looking animal. How do you tell his head from his tail?"

"Simple," said Dick, "you pull his tail and if it bites, you know it was his head."

* * *

"I once had a lap dog but I had to get rid of him."

"Why?"

"Every time I sat on his lap he bit me."

* * *

Did you ever notice how dogs win friends and influence people without reading books about it?

* * *

The Bostwicks moved from Chicago to the suburbs of Lincolnwood, and were advised to get a watchdog to guard the premises. They went to a nearby kennel and bought a very large dog.

Two weeks later the house was entered by thieves who made a good haul while the dog slept. Bostwick went to the kennel's owner and told him about it.

"What you need now," explained the owner, "is a little dog to wake up the big dog."

* * *

"I used to be in politics myself. I was a dogcatcher in my town for two years, but I finally lost the job."

"What happened? A new mayor?"

"No. I finally caught the dog."

*   *   *

"Is Rex a good watchdog?"

"He's great! Last week he watched somebody steal the lawn mower, then he watched the garage burn down, then he watched . . ."

*   *   *

"I thought you said he was a good watchdog!"

"Well, isn't he?"

"Certainly not. Last night he barked so loud that burglars came and went without our hearing them."

*   *   *

Mrs. Bishchoff was eating at a swanky restaurant with her young son. The boy hardly touched his dinner and so she called the waiter and said, "Wrap up these roast beef leftovers for the dog, please."

"Gee, Mom," exclaimed the child, "are we gonna get a dog?"

*   *   *

Until just recently, an Alabama postman delivered mail to his back-country route on a donkey. One morning a mongrel dog ran out from behind a house barking loudly.

The burro reached down and chomped his teeth into the mongrel's leg. This stands as the only case on record where a mailman's ass bit a dog.

* * *

"What's wrong with that dog of yours? Every time I go near the water cooler, he growls."

"He won't bother you."

"Then what's he growling for?"

"He's mad because you're drinking out of his cup."

* * *

"But why did you buy a dachshund for the children?"

"So that they can all pet him at once."

* * *

"I'm trying something new," the young mother was saying. "This year I'm sending my dogs to camp and my kids to obedience school."

* * *

Tony Poulos, Wyoming's premier saloon proprietor, wins customers with this whopper:

The veterinarian was elected sheriff and he continued his regular profession. One night a woman phoned him, asking him to hurry over to her home.

"Do you want me as sheriff or as vet?"

"Both. I want you to open up my bulldog's mouth—he's got a burglar in it."

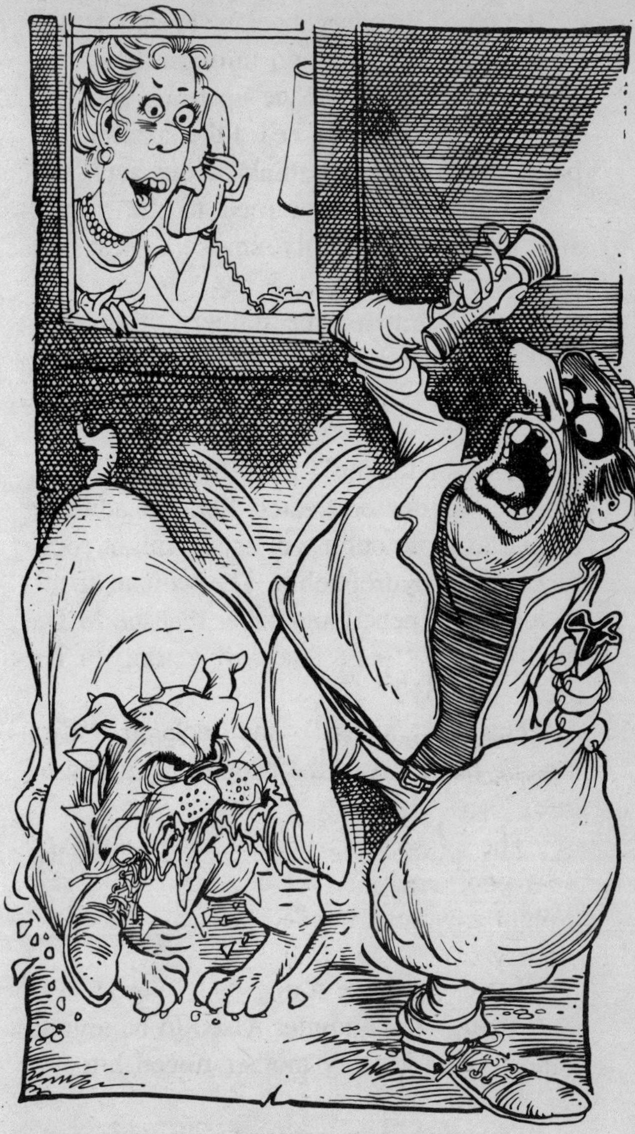

The bored Broadway booking agent watched two performing dogs go through their routine. His mind was made up to dismiss the act when he suddenly heard the smaller dog bark, "What do you think of our act?"

The startled agent turned to the trainer and exclaimed, "Holy smoke, does that little dog talk?"

"Naw," drawled the trainer, "the other mutt's a ventriloquist."

* * *

Dulcie had been bitten by a dog. Although the doctor treated her, he advised Dulcie to write out a will as she might soon succumb to hydrophobia. The woman spent so long with pencil and paper that the M.D. finally said, "Isn't that will getting to be pretty lengthy?"

"This isn't a will!" she declared. "I'm writing out a list of the people I'm going to bite."

* * *

"I see you have a dog."

"Yeah, he's a pointer. Used to be a good hunting dog but my mother ruined him."

"How?"

"She taught him it wasn't polite to point."

*   *   *

Buck returned from obedience school and was asked by his owner, "Did you learn to add and subtract today?"

The dog shook his head.

"Did you learn how to write?"

Again Buck shook his head.

"Did you learn how to read?"

Once more he shook his head.

"Did you learn any foreign languages?"

The dog replied, "Meow!"

*   *   *

"It's raining cats and dogs."

"I know. I just stepped into a poodle outside."

*   *   *

Courtland was from Cleveland and never had gone hunting before. Zack, a country friend, provided the dogs to accompany him. Courtland started early in the morning, only to return in about an hour.

"Why are you back so soon?" asked Zack.

"I'm after more dogs," he replied.

"More dogs?" repeated his friend. "Those were good dogs I gave you."

"I know, but I shot them all already."

*   *   *

Why did the guy call his dog Herpes?
Because he wouldn't heel.

* * *

"Saul has a great new watchdog!"
"What's so great about him?"
"At any suspicious noise Saul gets up, wakes the dog, and the dog begins to bark."

* * *

"Don't you like dogs?"
"I had a dog once. He got fleas. So I bought him a lovely hand-rubbed solid-mahogany flea collar. Then he got termites."

* * *

A Milwaukee couple sent their boy to camp for the summer. They didn't hear from him. After three weeks the mother phoned long distance and got the boy on the phone. "Are you all right, Neville?"

"Yep," answered the boy.

"Are you homesick?" asked the mother.

"Nope."

The woman was devastated. "Well," she asked, "aren't any of the other boys homesick?"

"No," said Neville. "Only the ones with dogs."

*   *   *

"Why do people give their dogs such weird names?"

"I don't know. We call our dog 'Handy' because he keeps doing odd jobs around the house."

*   *   *

Dolly, the dachshund, put her nose next to Phillipe, the French poodle, and said, "Listen, weirdo, I don't want to do it 'human style,' and if you suggest it again I'll call the cops."

*   *   *

Dr. Brad Stuart, the consummate California internist, perks up patients with this mirthful medicine:

Margi, the magician's assistant, was a very shapely blonde in her snug-fitting costume. As the magician began sawing her in half, he explained to the audience:

"After the performance, ladies and gentlemen, the young lady's brain will be given to science and, so there will be no waste, the rest will be thrown to the dogs."

From the back of the theatre a voice shouted, "Woof, woof!"

Beldon came home from work and spotted a gorilla on the roof of his house. He looked up "Gorilla Removal," in the Yellow Pages and called "Gordon's Gorilla-Removal Service."

Gordon arrived bringing bananas, a ladder, a large net, a gun, and a German shepherd. "What are you going to do?" asked Beldon.

"Well," said Gordon, "I'm gonna throw the banana up to the gorilla and while he's peeling and eating it, I'll sneak up the ladder to the roof behind him. When I push him off the roof, the German shepherd is trained to bite him where it hurts most, and when the gorilla grabs himself in pain, you throw the net over him."

"But, why the gun?" asked Beldon.

"If I miss the gorilla and fall off the roof myself, you shoot the dog!"

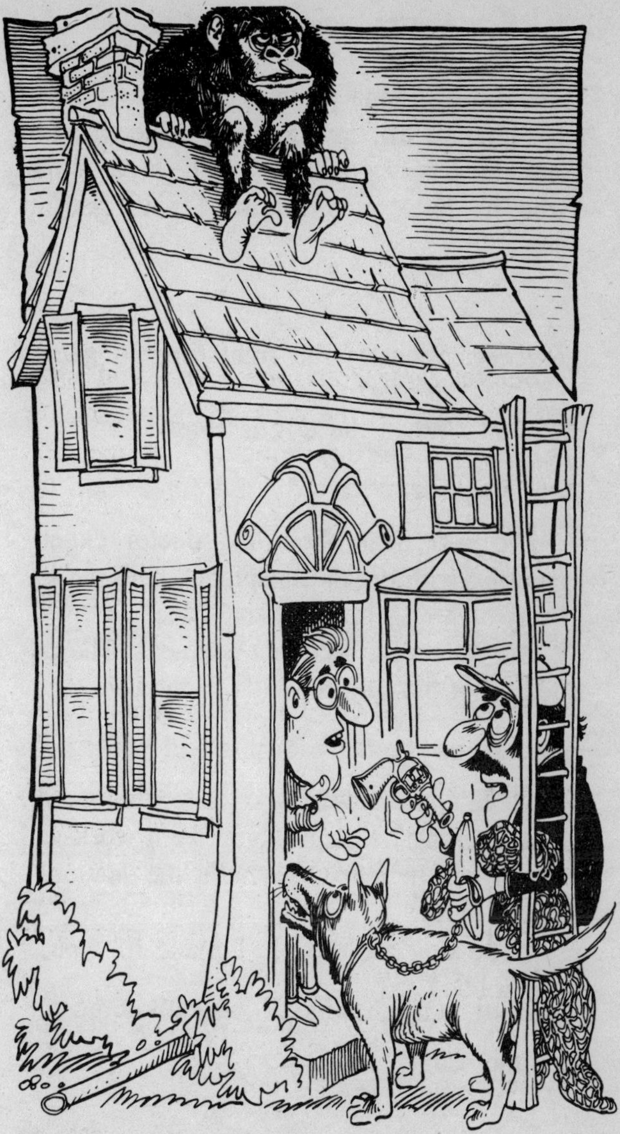

"Hey, mister, your dog just bit me."

"He did not."

"You're gonna prove it."

"First of all, my dog has no teeth; second, he's very gentle; third, he's particular who he bites; and fourth, I ain't got no dog."

* * *

Teacher: What is the right time to gather apples?

Buster: When the dog is chained up.

* * *

Did you hear about the doctor experimenting with organ transplants, who put the heart of a dog in a patient?

But he couldn't collect payment. The patient kept burying the bills in his backyard.

* * *

Steve's new wife was a terrible cook. One evening he came home from work and found her in tears. "What's the matter?" asked Steve.

"The dog ate the pie I made for you," she sobbed.

"Don't worry," said Steve. "I'll buy you another dog."

* * *

Walt and Ozzie were discussing marital infidelity. "What would you do," asked Walt, "if you found your wife in bed with another man?"

"What would I do if I found my wife in bed with someone else? Why I'd break the son of a bitch's white cane and shoot his dog!"

* * *

Sal showed up at work with a black eye and a puffed lip. "What happened to you?" asked a friend.

"I was out walking the dog last night," explained Sal, "and I met this real hot lookin' blonde. She says to me, 'Would you like to see my cute little schnauzer?' and I said, 'No thanks, I'm happily married,' and so she slugged me."

* * *

Eddie met Jessica, a pretty flight attendant, at a singles bar. After a few drinks, he said, "Let's go back to my pad. My dog Prince can make drinks, and he does great tricks with girls!"

"Hold it!" snapped Jessica. "I don't go that route."

Three wine coolers later, the stewardess relented and they went to Eddie's apartment. His dog Prince fixed them vodka martinis. "My," said Jessica, "ain't he clever." In twenty minutes, Prince prepared two more.

Feeling pretty good now, Jessica said, "What about those tricks your dog does with girls?"

"Just pop in the bedroom with Prince," said Eddie, "and take off your clothes."

In they went. Ten minutes later, Eddie followed. The girl lay naked on the bed—Prince sat on the dresser peering out the window. "You said your dog did great tricks with girls in bed," exclaimed Jessica. "He hasn't done a thing!"

"Damn it, Prince!" said Eddie removing his jacket and then his shirt. "I'm gonna show you this trick only one more time!"

Chicken Chuckles

How do you guard against offending your pet chicken?

Never use any four letter obscenities like soup, boil, bake, or cook.

*　　*　　*

What do you get if you cross a hen with a silkworm?

A chicken that lays eggs with panty hose inside.

*　　*　　*

What do you call it when a chicken cheats at cards?

Fowl play.

*　　*　　*

"If you feed hens different foods it will affect the eggs," explained the agricultural adviser to farmer Holtz.

"I know that," replied Holtz. "A cousin of mine in Texas fed his hens sawdust, and when the eggs were hatched, six of the chickens had wooden legs and four of them were woodpeckers."

*   *   *

Did you hear about the rooster that got caught in a rainstorm so he made a duck under the barn?

*   *   *

IN PERSONAL COLUMN OF RURAL WEEKLY

Anyone found near my
chicken house at night
will be found there next morning.

*   *   *

Morrow was driving down a Mississippi country road when he hit a wandering cock. He stopped and went back to the farmhouse. "I'm afraid I killed your cock, ma'am, but I'd very much like to replace him."

"Okay," said the farmer's wife. "Go around the house, you'll find the hens in the back."

*   *   *

There was a fire during the night in a Baltimore apartment house. All the tenants ran out into the street, scantily clad and carrying their prize possessions. Justine, an advertising exec, noticed that the man who lived directly above her was carrying a covered cage.

"What have you got in that cage?" she asked.

"That's my pet rooster," he answered, uncovering the cage.

"My God!" screamed Justine. "I've been going to a shrink for a year because I kept hearing roosters crowing."

*   *   *

"Well, how do you want your egg this morning?" said the rooster to the hen.

*   *   *

CHICKEN

The only animal you can eat before it's born and after it's dead.

*   *   *

And then there's the one about the cross-eyed rooster chasing two hens. "Gosh," said one hen to the other, "we'd better slow down or he'll miss both of us!"

*   *   *

Farmer Larson decided that his rooster was getting old and that he'd better buy a new young one. He got to town and went to see the local poultry dealer. "What're you askin' for a nice, strong, healthy, and prolific rooster?" asked Larson.

"Well," said the dealer, "we have 'em for thirty, forty, and fifty dollars, but you can't beat the seventy-five dollar one. It's guaranteed!"

"Well," said the farmer, "that's quite a bit of money, but I'll take the seventy-five-dollar rooster on your recommendation."

Larson got the rooster home and let him loose in the chicken coop. Inside, the new rooster saw the old rooster and decided to show him who was going to be boss. The old rooster was afraid of this new strong one, so he started running away from him. As the new rooster chased him across the yard, Larson saw his beautiful new expensive rooster running after the old one and fumed, "How do ya like that? I paid seventy-five dollars for a fairy!"

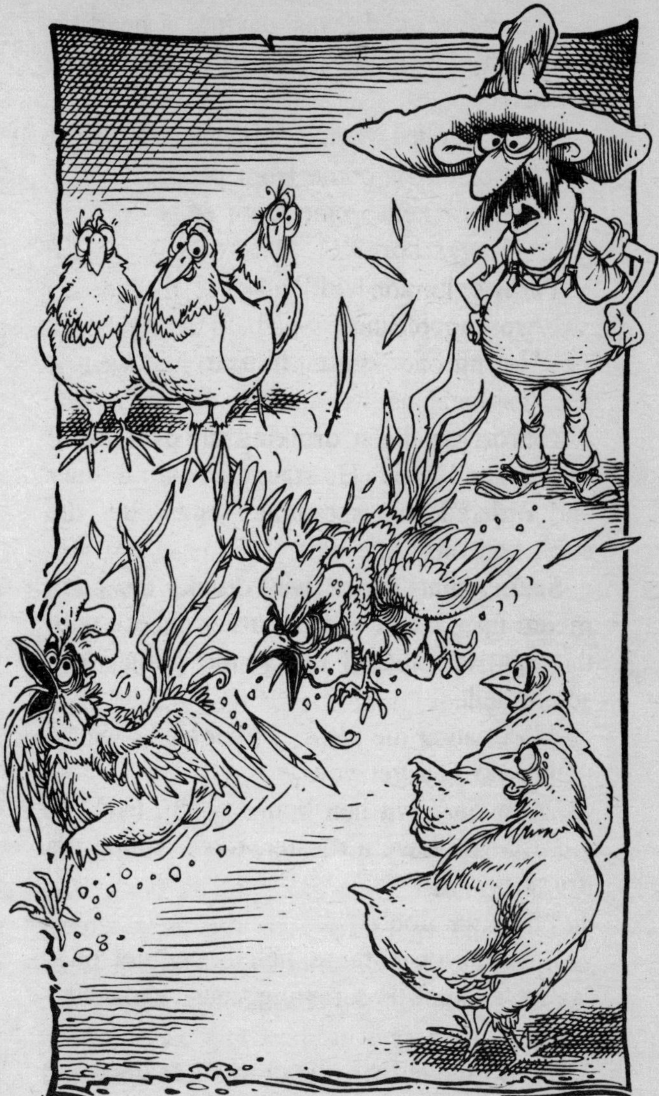

The baby chick was having a heart-to-heart with her mother. "Am I people?" she asked.

"No," replied Mama. "You are a chicken."

"Do chickens come from people?"

"No, chickens come from eggs."

"Are eggs born?"

"No, eggs are laid."

"Are people laid?"

"Not all. Some are chicken."

* * *

Trevor had been drinking all evening at the corner saloon. He staggered into a diner and ordered two scrambled eggs, but the cook had only one egg.

Seeing that Trevor was drunk, the cook mixed up a batch of Limburger cheese with the egg and served the whole thing well-scrambled.

After eating the mess, Trevor said, "Shay, where do you get your eggs?"

"Got our own hen house out in back."

"Do you have a rooster, too?" asked the drunk.

"No, we don't."

"Well, you sure as hell better get one, 'cause a skunk is screwing your chickens!"

* * *

Which came first, the chicken or the egg? Neither. The cock came first.

* * *

CHICKEN DELIGHT

One hen with two roosters.

*   *   *

Sterling decided to throw a party for twelve friends and wanted to serve each of his guests a separate roast chicken. He drove out to a local poultry breeder and told him to create twelve chickens for the party that night. The poultry man went to his barn and discovered he only had eleven chickens, so he put an old parrot into the coop with them.

The coop was loaded on the back of Sterling's car. As he was nearing home, Sterling suddenly heard a burst of cackling from the rear. He saw eleven chickens running alongside the moving auto. Then he noticed the parrot for the first time. The old bird was leaning out of the coop, calling to the chickens, "When you old hens decide to be reasonable, you can all get back in the car."

Parrot Pranks

Shanda, a very high-class lady of the evening, died and all her worldly possessions, including a parrot, were being auctioned off.

"What am I offered for this beautiful bird?" cried the auctioneer.

"Twenty-five dollars," bid a bystander.

"Fifty dollars!" roared another.

"Make it a hundred, Daddy," squawked the parrot, "and I'll be 'specially nice to you."

* * *

Old Auntie Maude returned to Proctor's Pet Shop and complained to the owner.

"This parrot I bought yesterday uses profane language."

"Well, maybe he does swear a little," admitted Proctor, "but you ought to be thankful that he doesn't drink, smoke, or gamble."

      *   *   *

Phyllis approached the clerk in a St. Louis Pet Shop and said, "My husband is away so much of the time, I want a parrot for company. Does this one use rough language?"

"Lady, with this bird in the house you'll never miss your husband."

      *   *   *

What would you call a parrot that eats beans?
A Thunderbird!"

      *   *   *

Old Mrs. Van Horn inherited Penrod, a parrot that used a lot of dirty words. After a number of embarrassing experiences, she told the minister about her problem.

"I have a female parrot," suggested the preacher, "who is an absolute saint. She sits on her perch and prays from morning till night. Suppose you bring your parrot over. My bird will have a good influence over him."

Mrs. Van Horn brought Penrod over to the minister's home. When the two cages were placed together, the parrots looked at each other for a while in silence. Finally Penrod cried, "Hello, baby, how about a little loving?"

"Great!" cried the female parrot. "That's just what I've been praying for all these years."

* * *

Looking around in a pet shop, a lady wandered over to a parakeet's cage. "Can you talk?" asked the woman.

"Sure," replied the bird, "can you fly?"

* * *

Kaplan had two parrots. He brought them to a pet shop so he could find out which was the male and which was female. Kaplan met a man in the shop who said, "I'm a bird expert and I can tell you."

"I'd appreciate that."

"If you'll notice every time the birds eat worms," said the man, "the male bird always eats the male worms and the female bird eats the female worms."

"Well," said Kaplan, "how do you know which is the male and which is the female worm?"

"I don't know that. I'm just a bird expert."

* * *

All the parrots at Garver's Pet Shop had been sold, so the owner suggested that the customer buy a woodpecker instead.

"But can he talk?" asked the customer.

"No, but if you understand Morse code, he'll give you a lot of fun."

*　　*　　*

Amy's parrot Quentin embarrassed her whenever she came into the apartment with a man. Quentin would shout obscenities, starting with "Somebody's gonna get it tonight! Somebody's gonna get it tonight!"

Amy went to a pet shop for help.

"You need a female parrot too," said the owner. "I don't have one, but I'll order it. Meanwhile, you could borrow this female owl."

Amy took the owl home and put it near her parrot. Quentin didn't care for the owl at all.

That evening Amy brought home a new boyfriend and as she opened the door, the parrot screeched, "Somebody's gonna get it tonight! Somebody's gonna get it tonight!"

The owl said, "Whooo? Whooo?"

"Not you, you goggle-eyed freak!" said the parrot. "I can't stand women who wear glasses!"

*　　*　　*

Jessica never married. As the years passed and she remained a spinster, her constant companion remained Plato the parrot. Figuring the bird might be getting lonely, she went out, bought a little canary, and put it in a cage next to Plato.

"Peep-peep!" said the little canary.

"I already peeped," said the parrot, "and it ain't worth it."

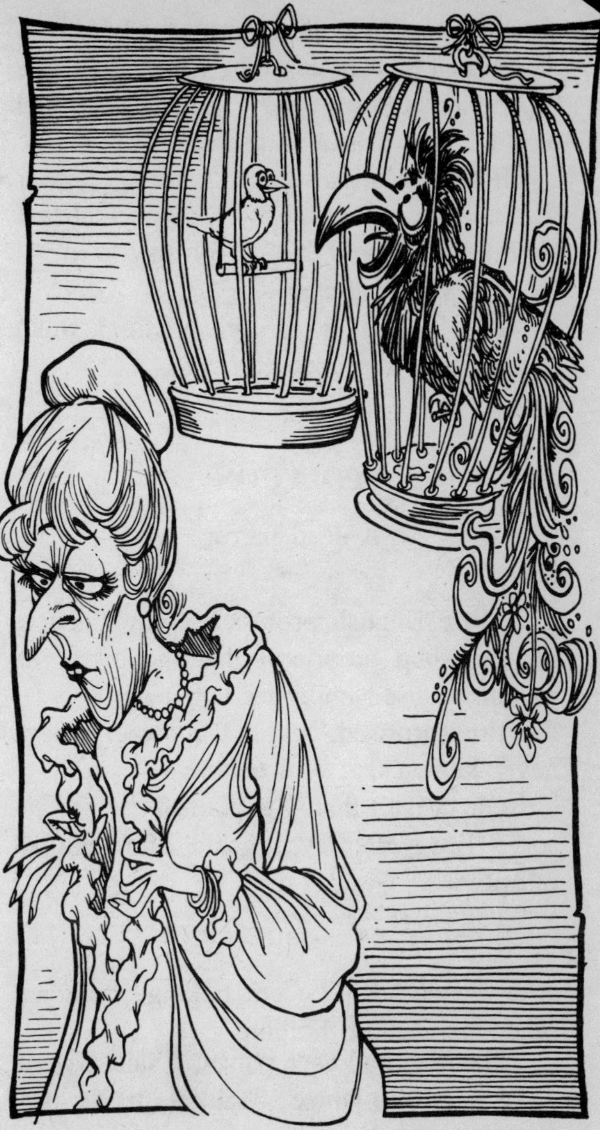

Foster sent his wife a parrot for her birthday. When he arrived home from a business trip he asked her, "How did you like that parrot I gave you as a present?"

"It was delicious."

"You mean you ate it? Do you realize I paid five hundred bucks for that bird? It spoke seven languages."

"Then why didn't it say something when I put him in the oven?"

*   *   *

POLYGON

A dead parrot.

*   *   *

A Yale English professor complained to the pet shop proprietor that the parrot he purchased used improper language.

"I'm surprised," said the owner. "I've never known that bird to swear."

"Oh, it isn't that," explained the professor. "But yesterday I heard him split an infinitive."

*   *   *

Gwen and Holli were talking about another member in the club.

"She's as bad as a parrot," said Gwen.

"She's even worse," said Holli. "A par-

40

rot doesn't hunt you up and force you to listen.''

*　　*　　*

Joy got out of bed,
Put on her robe,
Put on the shade,
Uncovered the parrot,
Went to the kitchen,
Lit the gas,
Put on the coffee,
And the telephone rang.
''Hi-ya, Babe, just got into town.
Get ready. I'll be right over.''
Joy took off the coffee,
Turned off the gas,
Went into the bedroom,
Pulled down the shade,
Covered the parrot,
Took off the robe,
Got in the bed,
And the parrot said,
''Wow what a short day, that was!''

*　　*　　*

What does a five-hundred-pound parrot say?
Polly wants a cracker—NOW!

*　　*　　*

Mrs. Anderson bought a parrot but could not get it to talk. The family tried everything, beginning with "Polly want a cracker?" but with no result. That afternoon at her bridge party, the discussion turned to silk underwear.

"Look at this lovely slip," said Mrs. Green turning up the corner of her dress.

"And look at these cute panties," said Mrs. Hall, pulling up her skirt all the way.

"Home at last!" shouted the parrot. "One of you whores give me a cigarette!"

*　　*　　*

Barbara went into a pet shop to buy a parrot.

"Here's a fine talking bird," said the salesman. "For years he was kept in the office of a big movie producer. Weren't you, Polly?"

"Yes, sir," shrilled the parrot. "Yes, yes, oh, yes, sir. Yes, indeed! You're absolutely right. Yes, sir!"

*　　*　　*

"My, what a big canary!"

"That's not a canary. That's my parrot. He has yellow jaundice."

*　　*　　*

Jim Schroder, the blissful Best Western Inn proprietor, beams over this bubbling bauble:

Once upon a time there was a parrot who could say only three words: "Who is it?" One day when the parrot was alone in the house, there was a loud knock on the door. "Who is it?" screeched the parrot. "It's the plumber," said the visitor.

"Who is it?" repeated the parrot.

"It's the plumber!"

"Who is it?"

"It's the plumber! You phoned me that your cellar was flooded."

Again the parrot called, "Who is it?"

The plumber became so angry he had a heart attack and keeled over dead. Two neighbors rushed over to see the cause for the commotion and found him on the floor. One neighbor asked, "Who is it?"

The parrot squawked, "It's the plumber!"

*   *   *

A spinster and a sailor's parrot were the only two survivors of a shipwreck, and they'd been clinging to a piece of driftwood for days. "How's your wrinkled old ass?" croaked the parrot.

"Oh, shut up!" snapped the old maid.

"Mine, too," said the parrot. "Must be this damn saltwater."

*   *   *

Blalock always wanted to own a parrot and when he noticed the sign BANKRUPT-CY SALE on a pet shop, he thought he might get one reasonably. Entering, he saw a gorgeous parrot in a cage. When the auctioneer put it up for sale he began bidding; higher and higher went the bids, but finally the parrot was his.

Bursting with pride of ownership, Blalock carried the parrot home in its cage. "Okay, now talk to me," he said.

The parrot said nothing.

"C'mon, now, say something."

Silence.

"Good heavens," cried Blalock, "I paid five hundred bucks for you, and you can't even talk!"

"Can't talk?" echoed the parrot. "Who the hell you think was bidding against you?"

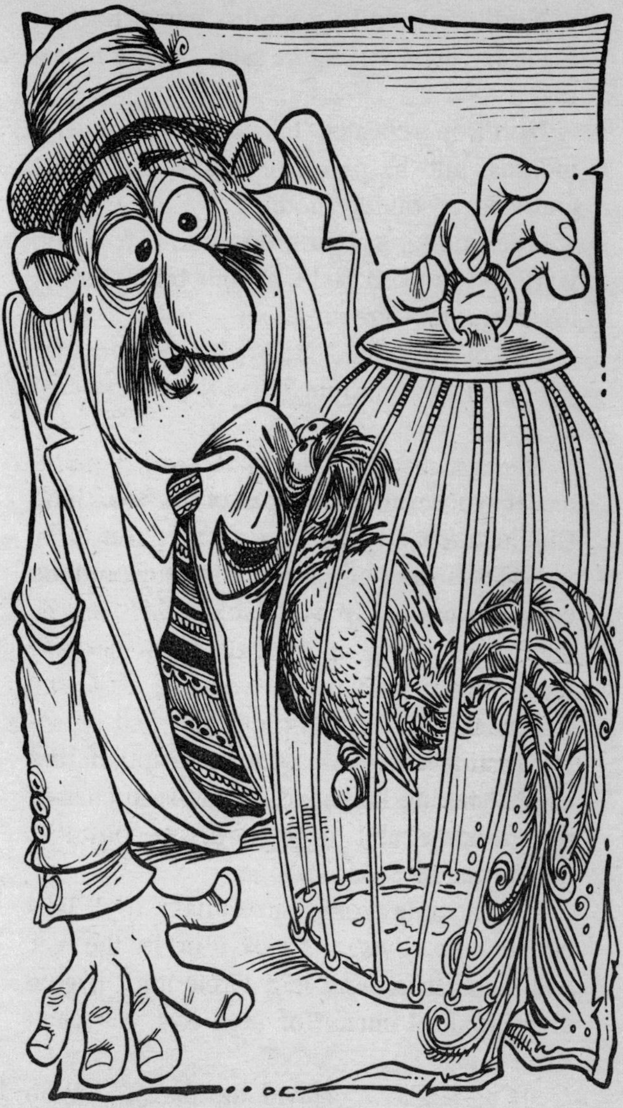

Northrop tried to teach his parrot to talk. Each day upon arising he said, "Good morning!" to it.

Northrop repeated his effort for several months, but the parrot refused to cooperate and said absolutely nothing.

One morning Northrop didn't feel too well and walked right by the bird without his customary greeting.

The parrot said, "Hey, what's the matter with you this morning?"

* * *

"If you want your parrot to talk, you should begin by teaching it short words."

"That's strange. I thought it would be easier to teach it polysyllables."

* * *

Penelope, a Vermont spinster, had a parrot formerly owned by a sea captain that used shocking language. Anxious to change the speaking habits of the bird, she consulted the owner of a pet shop.

"Next time your parrot uses foul language," he advised, "pick it up by the feet and swing it around in a circle until it gets dizzy. That'll cure it of the habit."

Next day, when the bird swore as usual, Penelope picked it up and swung it around and around. Then she put it down.

The parrot staggered away and yawped, "Dammit! What a breeze!"

* * *

Farley walked into Porter's Pet Shop and saw a parrot he liked.

"How much," he asked.

"That's a very special parrot," said Porter. "It's three thousand dollars."

"What's so special about it?"

"She's the only parrot in America that lays square eggs!"

"Square eggs?"

"Yes," said the Porter, and he showed him a dish of eggs, each a perfect cube.

"Okay," said Farley, "I'll take the bird with me." While the bill was being written up Farley said, "I suppose the parrot can talk?"

"She can," said the owner, "but so far she only seems to have one expression."

"What's that?"

"Ooooo Ooooo Kee-rist!"

* * *

"What's smarter—a parrot or a chicken?"

"I don't know."

"Think about it—have you ever heard of Kentucky Fried Parrot?"

* * *

Old Mrs. Carmichel kept a parrot for years and years, but try as she would, she was unable to make it talk. Even though the parrot never spoke, the widow still looked after its needs. One day Mrs. Carmichel was feeding it a carrot when the bird roared out, "There's a worm in it. There's a worm in it."

"You can talk!" she exclaimed. "Why haven't you spoken in all the years I've had you?"

"Up to now," said the parrot, "the food has been excellent."

* * *

A new species appeared in the local pet shop. Sawyer went to investigate and came home to report to his wife.

"What is it?" she asked.

"A cross between a parrot and a tiger."

"Does it talk?"

"Only a little. But when it does say something, you'd better listen."

* * *

Rojek saw a parrot in a tree and he began to climb up after it. The parrot climbed higher and higher, with Rojek in pursuit. When the bird reached the topmost branch, it suddenly whipped around and screeched, "What do you want?"

"Excuse me, mister," said the Pole, "I thought you were a bird."

Hyacinth stormed into the pet shop and cornered the owner. "How dare you," she screamed. "You sold me a parrot and you told me it could speak five languages, that it would be a perfect companion for me. I've had that parrot for a week and he hasn't even opened his mouth. What do you mean by selling me a bird like that? I paid you my hard earned money in order to get a parrot that could talk. And do you realize that he hasn't said one word yet, and—"

"Lady," interrupted the owner, "give the poor bird a chance."

* * *

The police raided a bordello and among the property confiscated was an unusually talkative parrot. They turned the bird over to an animal shelter, which in turn gave it to a society matron.

The bird and cage arrived at the woman's home one afternoon while she was giving a charity tea for some local bigwigs. When she uncovered the cage, the bird blinked, looked around at the women and said, "Ah, a new crop of girls."

The socialite began to coax the bird to talk more. "Ah, a new madam," said the parrot. Then looking around at the men, squawked, "Oops, same old customers."

* * *

Mrs. Thompson loved her parrot Newton. At her dinner parties, Newton was the center of attention, for he repeated what the butler said when he announced the arriving guests. Unfortunately, every chance he got, Newton would fly over the fence into farmer Franklin's nearby yard and screw his chickens.

Franklin complained to Mrs. Thompson and she laid the law down to the parrot. "Newton," she said, "next time you fornicate with those chickens, I'm going to punish you."

Two days later, over the fence he went and the farmer again complained. As punishment, Mrs. Thompson clipped all the feathers from the top of the parrot's head— he was totally bald.

That night Mrs. Thompson had a party and she put the parrot on the piano. "Newton," she said, "you're to sit here all night!"

While Newton sat on the piano, the butler announced the guests and he repeated the names.

Then two bald-headed men entered and Newton shouted, "All right, you chicken chasers! Up here on the piano with me!"

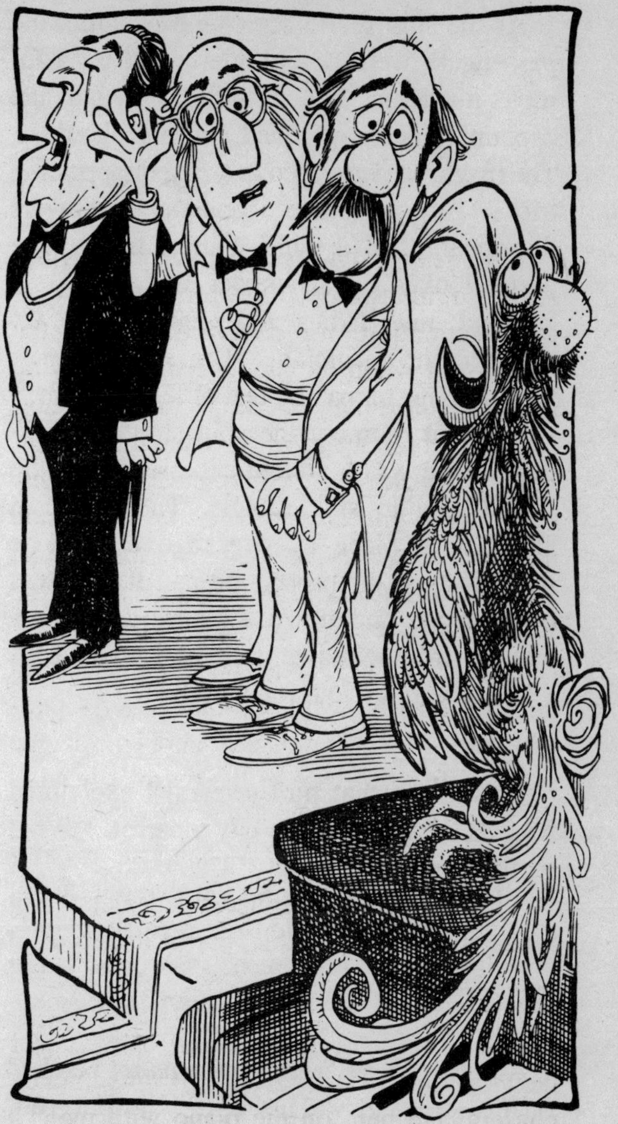

As the ship sailed across the Atlantic, the passengers were being entertained by a famous magician. Watching the show was the captain's parrot perched on his shoulder. The magician performed amazing disappearing tricks. First he made a bouquet of flowers disappear, then a table, then a trunk. The parrot looked on in wonder and awe.

"And now, ladies and gentlemen," announced the magician, "I'm about to perform my most amazing feat of legerdemain."

At that moment the ship struck an iceberg, there was a violent explosion, and the ship began to sink rapidly. The magician clung to a piece of wreckage and as he floated along, he passed the parrot who was bobbing up and down on a wooden spar. The parrot looked at him and squawked, "You and your lousy magic."

*　　*　　*

"Oh, how that bird swears!" exclaimed Mrs. Edelman about to buy a parrot. "What would my husband say?"

"I don't know," replied the dealer. "But whatever he says, this parrot'll repeat it right after him."

*　　*　　*

Mooky entered a bar with a parrot perched on his shoulder. "This bird," he bragged, "speaks five languages."

"Go'wan," said the barkeep. "I'll bet you five to one he can't even talk English."

All the customers joined in the betting until there was a fortune lying on the bar. Mooky said to the parrot, "Okay, say something in French!"

No answer.

"Say something in Spanish!" Silence. "English!" Nothing. "Dutch!" Silence. "German!" More silence.

Mooky took the bird outside and started yelling at him. "You dope! We could've cleaned up at five to one. What made you so dumb all of a sudden?"

"I ain't dumb," said the parrot. "Wait 'til tomorrow, we'll get twenty to one!"

Jungle Jests

Why do gorillas have big nostrils?
Because their fingers are so big.

*　　*　　*

What's worse than a centipede with corns?
A giraffe with a sore throat.

*　　*　　*

Adeline and Isadora, two spinster monkeys, were chattering in the jungle. "Just look at that deer making a fool of herself for two bucks," said Adeline.

Isadora sighed. "I could use a little doe myself."

*　　*　　*

"Is it true," a reporter asked a safari guide, "that jungle animals won't harm you if you carry a torch?"

"That depends," replied the guide, "on how fast you carry it."

JUNGLE VIRGIN

A monkey whose monkey has
never been monkeyed with.

*   *   *

When the caveman started writing with flint and chisel, someone shouted to him, "Hey! Hurry! A saber-toothed tiger is fighting with your mother-in-law!"

"All right, let 'em fight," said the caveman. "What do I care what happens to a saber-toothed tiger."

*   *   *

In the jungle, a lion and a bull got into a ferocious struggle. The lion won, killed the bull, and ate it.

The lion, proud of himself, started roaring and continued roaring in triumph. The noise attracted a hunter who followed the sound until he located the lion. The hunter then killed the lion.

MORAL: When you are full of bull, it is best to keep your mouth shut.

*   *   *

Charlie Harper, Houston's newest celebrity resident, gets big ha-has with this humdinger:

Mervin, a horny monkey, was swinging through the trees hoping to find another monkey to fool around with. He couldn't find one. Weeks passed and he became desperate. One day, Mervin spotted a lion, jumped down, and humped her.

When the monkey finished, he ran away but the lion began chasing him. Mervin came to a clearing, and there was a park bench with a newspaper lying on it. Mervin grabbed the paper and began reading it.

Suddenly the lion came running up and shouted, "Did you see a monkey go by here?"

"The one that screwed the lion?"

"My God!" shouted the lion, "you mean it's in the paper already?"

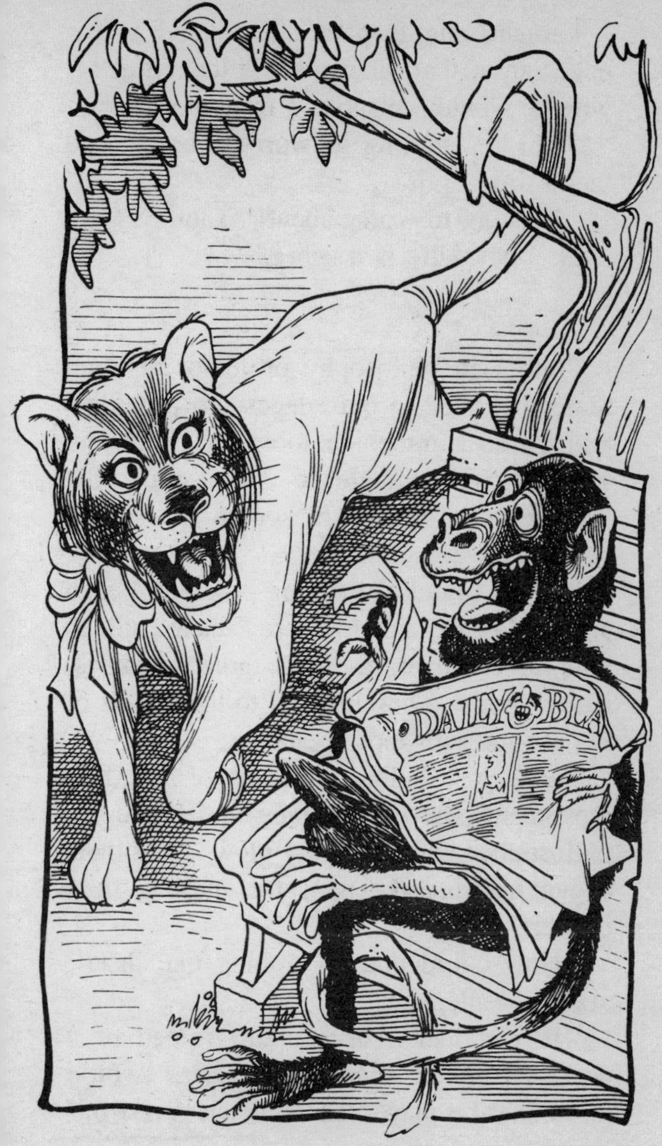
DAILY

Leonard the leopard complained to his psychiatrist that whenever he looked at his wife he would see spots in front of his eyes.

"This is nothing to worry about," said the shrink.

"Nothing to worry about!" shouted Leonard. "My wife is a zebra."

*   *   *

Philbin, a philosophy professor at Penn State, believed in old adages. To prove his point, one summer he took his violin and went into the jungle to demonstrate that "music hath charms to soothe the savage beast."

Philbin found a watering hole and began to play. Within minutes, there gathered around him an elephant, a tiger, three monkeys, and a giraffe. They listened to the strains of the sonata with rapt attention.

Then, just before the end of the first movement, the tiger sprang and killed the philosopher with a mighty blow. The others began berating the tiger for spoiling their concert.

"How could you do a thing like that?" asked the elephant.

"If you had a decent ear instead of a useless trunk," snarled the tiger, "you'd know that he played an A for an A-sharp."

*   *   *

What do female hippos say before sex?
"Can I be on top this time?"

*   *   *

A lion and a tiger drank beside a pool.
"Tell me, why do you roar like a fool?"
asked the tiger.

"That's not foolish," replied the lion.
"They call me king of all the beasts because I advertise."

A rabbit heard them talking and ran home like a streak. He thought he could try the lion's plan and began to roar. But his roar was a squeak. A fox heard the noise, came to investigate, and soon had his lunch.

MORAL: When you advertise, be sure you've got the goods!

*   *   *

"Daddy, why do giraffes have such long necks?"

"So they can feed off the tops of the trees."

"But why are the trees so high?"

"So that the giraffes can eat."

*   *   *

"Does the giraffe get a sore throat if he gets wet feet?"

"Yes, but not until the next week."

*   *   *

Teacher: What is the highest form of animal life?
Geraldo: The giraffe.

*   *   *

A Charleston high-school biology class had been studying how nature forced animals to adapt to the conditions under which they had to live.

"Now, who can tell me," questioned the teacher, "why the giraffe has such a long neck?"

"I can," volunteered Jenny Sue. "It's because his head is so far from his body."

*   *   *

Magumbo and Bawana, two African natives, were watching a leopard chase a missionary.

"Can you spot the winner?" asked Magumbo.

"The winner is spotted," replied Bawana.

*   *   *

A skunk, a giraffe, and a deer walked into a cocktail lounge and ordered three whiskeys. They drank them down and ordered three more. The barkeep poured the drinks, but was anxious about being paid because no money was in sight.

Five minutes later, they repeated their orders, finished the drinks, and started for the door.

"Wait," shouted the bartender. "Who's gonna pay for this?"

"I can't," said the skunk, "I only have a scent."

"I can't" said the deer, "I had a buck last week and I'm only expecting a little doe."

"Well," said the giraffe, "I guess the highballs are on me."

Kitty Cackles

"Why do you feed your cat malted milk?"

"I'm trying to make a Maltese out of her."

* * *

"Hey, Dad, there's a big black cat in the dining room."

"That's okay, son. Black cats are lucky."

"I'll say. This one just ate your dinner."

* * *

How did the tomcat find out he was a father?

His wife sent him a litter.

* * *

CAT

An animal that's so unpredictable, you can never tell in advance how it will ignore you the next time.

* * *

Miss Prudence, a spinster who was very fond of her faithful she-cat, left on a Caribbean cruise. Before her departure, Prudence instructed her sister:

"And don't forget to take good care of Cassie. Feed her regularly, and whatever you do, don't let her out at night."

A few weeks passed and her sister received a card which read:

"Having a wonderful time. Met an attractive man on the ship . . . P.S. Let the cat out at night."

* * *

Trumbolt: When I bought this cat, you told me he was good for mice. He doesn't even go near them.

Pet Shop Owner: Isn't that good for mice?

* * *

Thompson's wife ordered him to get rid of their cat. He put it in a basket and tromped through the woods for seven or eight miles. When he returned, Mrs. Thompson asked, "Did you lose the cat?"

"Lose it," he replied. "If I hadn't followed it, I wouldn't have found my way home."

*   *   *

Ruth found her neighbor's wife Sally in tears.

"What's the matter?" she asked.

"I'm worried about Paul," she answered. "He's been trying for a week to get rid of our cat. He finally decided to take her up in his plane and drop her over the side."

"Now, that's nothing to worry about."

"It certainly is," wept Sally. "Paul isn't home yet, but the cat is."

TOMCAT

A ball-bearing mousetrap.

*   *   *

The Ruckers lived in Connecticut. One day the cat got sick and died. There was no backyard to their apartment house in which to bury the cat, so Mr. Rucker wrapped it up in newspaper and took it with him on the train to work. His plan was to toss the bundle out the train window.

Rucker carefully deposited his bundle up

on the luggage rack over his seat. He soon struck up a conversation with a fellow commuter and forgot to toss it out of the window. Rucker took the package to his office, intending to dispose of it on his way home that evening. But again he forgot and Rucker still had the bundle under his arm when he arrived home. His wife scolded him and Rucker promised to take care of it the next day. But when he arrived home the following day still carrying the bundle, Mrs. Rucker was furious.

"You've got to get rid of that cat right now," she insisted. "Go down to the basement at once and put it in the furnace."

Rucker sheepishly obeyed. As he lifted the bundle from the table, it fell open—and there to his great surprise was a boiled ham!

*   *   *

Little Gary sat on the stoop, weeping. Old Mrs. Walker who lived down the street asked him what the trouble was.

"My mother's gone and drowned the kittens," he wailed.

"That's too bad," said the neighbor. "But may be she had to do it."

"No, she didn't," he cried. "She promised to let me drown them."

*   *   *

Cindy, a pretty Persian pussy, was walking down a Pittsburgh street trailed by her four kittens. Suddenly, Tully, the big tomcat, approached her.

"Hi'ya, honey," said Tully.

"Don't 'honey' me," snapped Cindy. "You told me we were only wrestling."

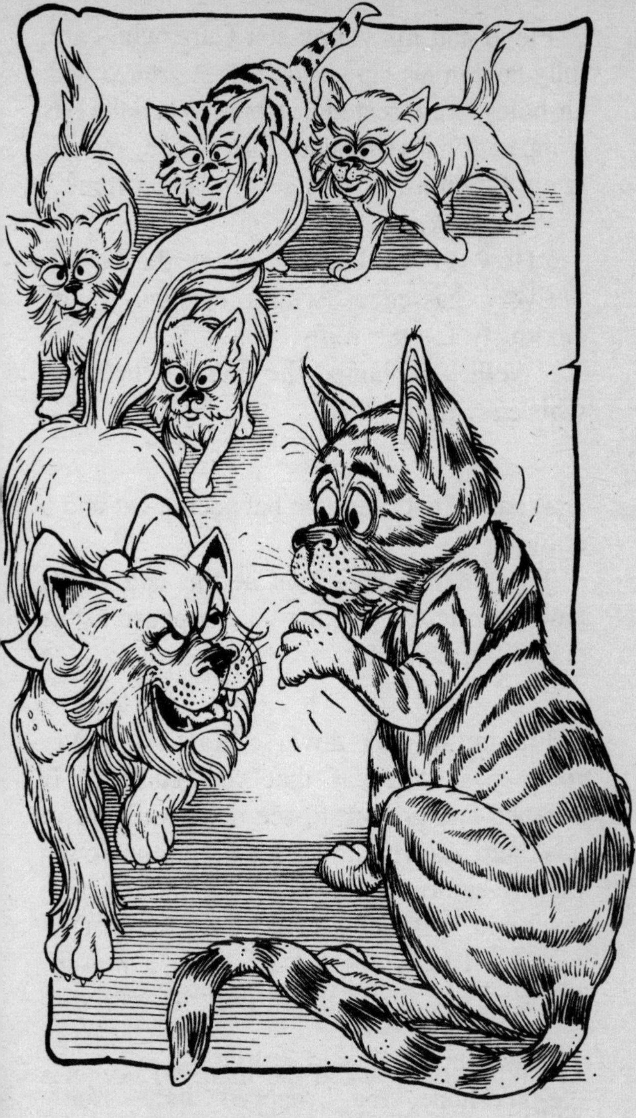

Floyd and his young son Curt, who carefully held in his lap a shoe box punctured with air holes, were seated in a bus. When the bus stopped for a red light, Curt asked, "Dad, is my kitten a man kitten or a lady kitten?"

"A man kitten," said Floyd.

"How do you know?" asked the boy.

Every passenger within earshot waited anxiously for the reply.

"Well," explained the father, "he's got whiskers, hasn't he?"

*　　*　　*

What's the difference between a cat and a comma?

The cat has its claws at the end of its paws, while the comma has its pause at the end of its clause.

*　　*　　*

Fulton, driving down a Kansas country road, passed a car that was stalled. He stopped and got out to see if he could be of any help. To his amazement, Fulton found the driver down in front of the car hitching up a pair of kittens to the front bumper.

"For Pete's sake!" exclaimed Fulton. "You're not gonna try to pull that car with those kittens?"

"Why not?" asked the man. "I've got a whip."

*　　*　　*

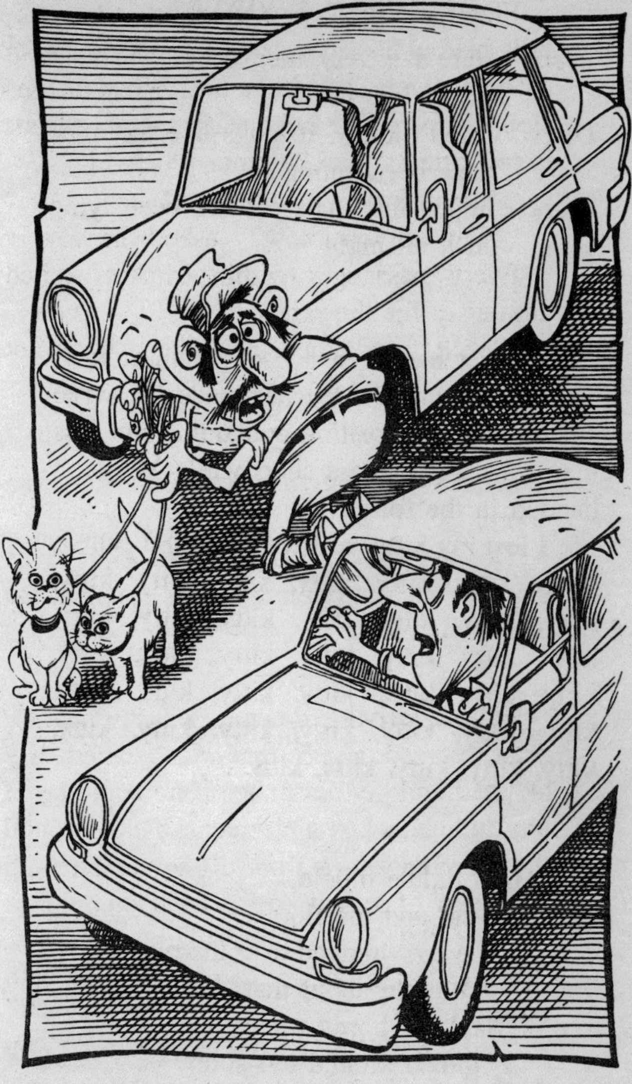

Clerk: Here's a very nice cake. I'm sure you'll like it.

Dixon: I don't know. It looks like the mice have been eating it.

Clerk: Impossible. The cat has been lying on it all night.

* * *

Margaret had been a bad girl in school. As punishment, the teacher made her write an original composition containing not less than fifty words. In a short while Margaret handed in the following:

"I lost my kitty, so I went out and called, 'Here kitty, kitty.' "

* * *

High diddle diddle,
The cat and the fiddle,
   The cow jumped over the moon.
   "Too bad about that,"
   Said the horny tomcat,
"I fiddled around too soon."

* * *

Did you hear about the Madison Avenue cat who's made so much money doing cat food commercials that he supports a family of six humans in high style?

And recently he bought his own tuna fishing fleet.

*   *   *

Jill: Your cat was making an awful noise last night.

Flo: Yes, ever since she ate your canary, she thinks she can sing.

*   *   *

Gardner, the marketing V.P. of a cat-food company, was addressing a sales meeting at the Newport Beach Ritz-Carlton, giving his men a pep talk.

"What cat food has more nutritional value than any other?" he asked.

"Ours!" roared the salesmen.

"What cat food maintains hospital sanitary standards?"

"Ours!"

"What cat food spends more money on research?"

"Ours!"

"Then why are we last in sales volume?"

A voice in the back cried, "Cats don't like it."

*   *   *

Monty the midget died. Friends came to pay their condolences and have a last look at the body lying in an upstairs room of the house. Walter, a close friend, came down and was asked by Monty's widow whether he had shut the door of the room where the body lay.

"No," said Walter. "I didn't think it was necessary."

"Then I'd better go up and shut it," said the widow. "The cat's had him downstairs twice already today."

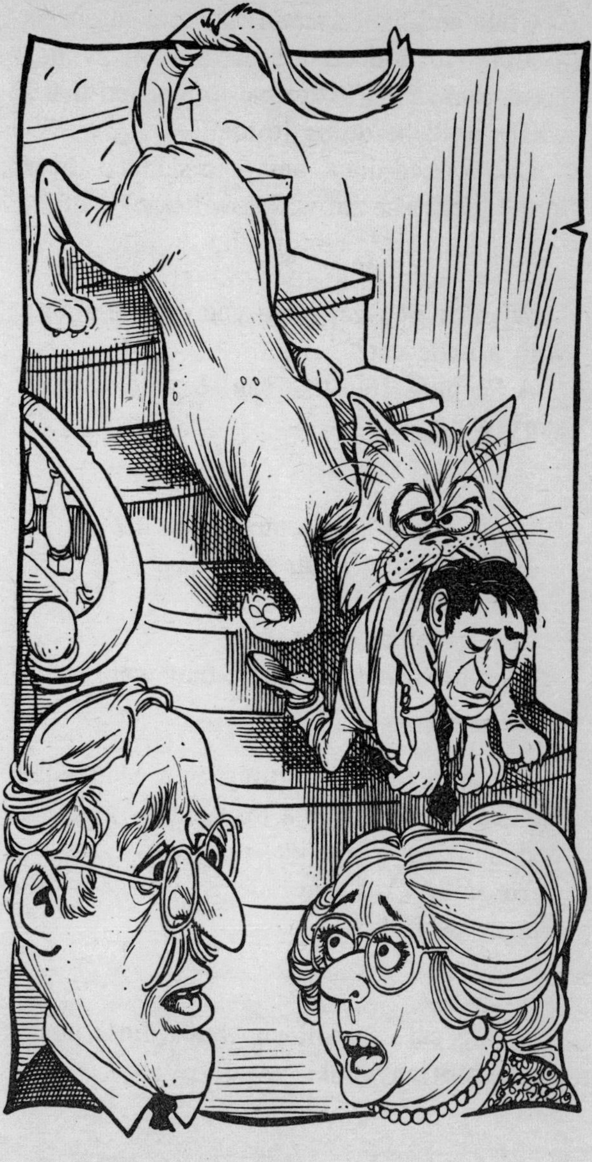

Craig and his fianceé Lisa were sitting on a sofa. He noticed the cat playing with a tassel and said, "After we're married that's what you'll be doing to me."

Lisa looked down and then slapped Craig in the face. The cat was now licking its tail.

*   *   *

What do you get when you cross a giraffe with a male cat?

A Peeping Tom that can see into second-story windows.

*   *   *

A wise and handsome young bat
Had a flitting affair with a cat
    But aerial sex
    Had lethal effects
And neither knew where they were at.

*   *   *

An attractive girl sitting at a Manhattan bar leaned across to a man sitting near her and said, "Do you like pussycats?"

He said, "Yes, but how did you know my name was Katz?"

*   *   *

A big cat can kill you but a little pussy never hurt anyone!

*   *   *

FELINE PHILOSOPHY

A catty remark often has more lives than a cat.

*   *   *

After Noah had assembled in his ark a pair of each species of animal, he got up and called everyone to order. "Due to cramped quarters and the uncertainty of the duration of the flood, there's to be no increase in any family. That would have to be postponed until the flood subsided and we're all on land again." Noah then appointed the giraffe to stand guard.

When the waters finally subsided, and the doors of the ark were flung open, out marched, as they had come in, two of each species—with one exception. The two cats came out with a litter of kittens. As they passed the giraffe, the male cat winked. "I'll bet," he remarked, "you thought we were only scrapping."

CAT OBEDIENCE SCHOOL

A place where they teach your pussy how to handle itself.

*   *   *

Ashes to ashes,
And dust to dust,
Show me a cat
That a mouse can trust.

* * *

The gift that keeps on giving: a pregnant cat.

* * *

Grandma Dovidov came from Russia to this country to live with her grandson Michael. The elderly widow loved America but she was keenly disappointed in not being able to learn the English language.

One day Michael's cat jumped on the table and helped herself to a plate of chopped liver.

"Upsheek! Upsheek!" Grandma yelled at the cat. But the cat, understanding not a word of Slavic cat-talk, didn't budge.

Michael, hearing the old woman's cries, rushed into the dining room and shouted, "Get the hell off the table!"

The cat jumped at once.

"Who would have ever thought," said the old woman in Russian, "that a plain cat would know more English than I."

"Whatsa matta? Cat got your tongue?"

What did the Texan say after his cat was run over by a steamroller?"

Nothing. He just stood there with a long puss.

* * *

What do you get when you cross a cat with a lemon?

A sourpuss.

* * *

CAT

A creature that never
cries over spilt milk.

* * *

Have you heard about the all-American tomcat that made forty-seven yards one night?

* * *

Monsieur La Farge with a talking Angora cat went to see a Broadway booking agent.

"Zis cat, she is extraordinaire," explained the Frenchman. "I 'ave taught her to speak ze Mother Goose. Leesten, and she recite."

The astonished theatrical agent listened as the Angora recited one nursery rhyme after another, all with a decided French accent. When the cat was finished, Monsieur La Farge beamed.

"Now," he asked, "how about ze contract?"

"Sorry, I can't use her," said the agent. "Not with that accent."

Canary Cuties

Benita spent nearly two hours inspecting the stock of linoleum in a shop. The perspiring salesman brought out roll after roll but still she was unsatisfied. He finally showed her the last roll and paused in despair.

"I'm sorry," he said, "but if you can wait I could get some more samples from the factory."

"Okay," she said, "and try to get something with very small designs, suitable for putting in the bottom of a canary's cage."

*   *   *

Did you hear about the careless canary who did it for a lark?

*   *   *

Two canaries in a cage. "Hey," said the male, "let's screw."

"No."

"Why not?"

"I've got chirpies."

*   *   *

What would you get if a canary got caught in the lawn mower?

Shredded tweet.

*   *   *

Halstead telephoned a warehouse for the price of a carload of canary birdseed. Later he asked if the same price would hold good on half a car. The manager assured him that it would.

Halstead called up again and wanted to know if the price would be the same on five hundred pounds.

"All right," agreed the manager.

Later Halstead called up and asked, "Would the same price hold good on one hundred pounds?"

"Listen," yelled the manager, "send your damn canary over here and we'll feed him for nothing."

*   *   *

John Cantu, the celebrated San Francisco comics coach, loves this show biz beaut:

Waverly entered a pet store and asked for a good singing canary. "I got a great one," said the owner. "This bird is a second Sinatra. He's worth two thousand dollars."

"Pretty steep," said the buyer, "but if he's that good, I'll take him."

"Oh, you can't buy him so easy," said the proprietor. "With him, you gotta take that other bird."

Waverly looked at a moldy old and ruffled bird, with rings under his eyes. "Why do I have to buy him?" he asked.

"Because," said the storekeeper, "he's the arranger."

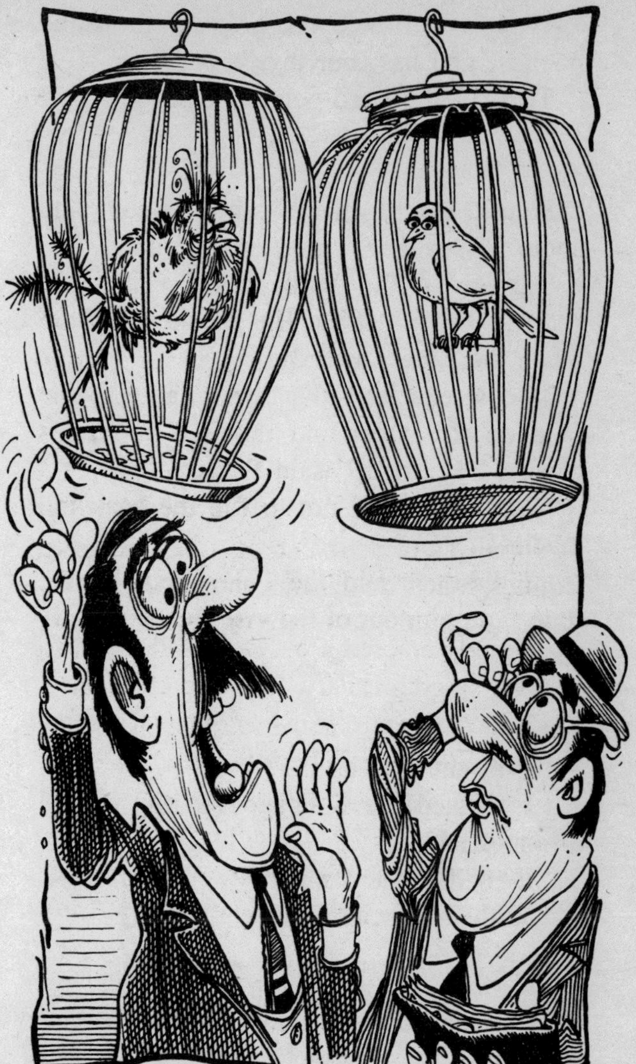

What's yellow, weighs one thousand pounds, and has four legs?

Two five-hundred-pound canaries.

* * *

Polaski went to the pet shop to complain about his canary who wouldn't sing. The owner said, "File the beak just a little bit, and the bird will sing. But if you file it too much the canary will die."

Two weeks later the owner ran into the Pole on the street and inquired about his canary. "He died," said Polaski.

"But I told you not to file the beak too much."

"I didn't," said the Pole, "but by the time I got him out of the vise, he be already dead."

* * *

"Why are you crying?"

"I cleaned the birdcage and the canary disappeared."

"How did you clean it?"

"With the vacuum cleaner."

* * *

What does a canary say when he finishes shopping?

Just put it on my bill.

* * *

Nelson walked into a pet shop and asked for a canary. "I got just the bird for you," said the owner. "He can sing 'Blue Moon', 'Stormy Weather,' and 'Old Black Magic.' "

"Don't try to palm off a phony on me," screamed the customer. "For my money I want a bird that can knock out original tunes!"

CANARY

A bird that's always going to seed.

* * *

Little Daphne was heartbroken when her pet canary died. To cheer the child, her father found an empty cigar box for the canary, and with much solemn ceremony assisted in burying it in the garden.

After the funeral, the little girl whispered, "Daddy, do you think my canary will go to heaven?"

"Of course he will," replied the father. "Why?"

"I was just thinking," said Daphne, "how angry St. Peter will be when he opens the box and finds there aren't any cigars in it."

* * *

What does a canary say at Halloween?
Trick or Tweet.

*   *   *

Why don't canaries fly on airplanes?
Because they are too cheep.

*   *   *

What has three eyes, three wings, and two bills?
A canary with spare parts.

*   *   *

Elderly Housewife: You say you were locked in a cage for ten years? Were you in prison, my good man?
Tramp (sarcastically): No, lady, I was a canary.

*   *   *

Francine, who lived alone in Chicago, asked her boyfriend Brett to buy her a pet for company. He found her a beautiful canary that sang light opera but unfortunately had only one leg. Francine loved the bird's voice, but couldn't bear to look at the poor thing standing on one leg. She begged Brett to trade it in for a two-legged bird. Next day he told the pet shop owner that his girl couldn't bear to see the pathetic creature on only one leg.

"If it's all right," said Brett, "I'd like to exchange this one for a bird with two legs."

"Whaddya want," asked the owner, "a singer or a dancer?"

Birds 'n' Bees Boffs

How did the bee break his leg?
He fell off his honey.

* * *

While Mrs. Fedaricci was walking down a Seattle street she noticed a going-out-of-business sign in a pet-store window. She dashed in and asked, "Do you have any birds left?"

"You are in luck, lady," replied the owner. "All the twitters is not sold." -

* * *

Did you hear about the bee that got mad because somebody took his honey and nectar?

* * *

NEWS ITEM

New York City Police today said they broke up a ring of killer bees that had been moonlighting as hit men for the Mafia. Taken into custody were 8 drones and 7 worker bees. The police are looking for one queen bee believed to be hiding out on Fire Island.

* * *

Seymour and Herbert, two sparrows, had agreed to meet at a large maple tree in Central Park. Seymour, whose regular beat was Westchester, flew down and landed in the appointed place with plenty of time to spare. He settled down to wait for his friend.

Hours passed, and Herbert did not appear. Seymour grew more and more distraught. Then, just as the sun was starting to set, Herbert appeared, woozy and shaken, with every feather awry.

"Good Lord!" exclaimed Seymour. "What's happened to you?"

"Oh, Lord!" replied Herbert. "I was flying here to meet you when I noticed a crowd at the other end of the park. I flew down to see what was happening and found myself caught in a badminton game!"

* * *

During the California gold rush a wealthy miner presented the city of San Francisco with a pair of statues to stand in Union Square. They were life-size, naked, obviously male and female, and they faced each other a few feet apart for a hundred years.

One night Venus, Goddess of Love, appeared to them and said: "For a hundred years you have faced each other with outstretched arms. I will reward your patience with any one wish you ask."

The man replied: "Will you make us human for just twenty-four hours, so that we may do what we have in mind?"

"At dawn you shall come alive," said Venus.

As promised they came alive and rushed into each other's arms. "How shall we begin?" said the woman.

"I know!" said the man. "I'll catch the pigeons in those nets, and you wring their necks."

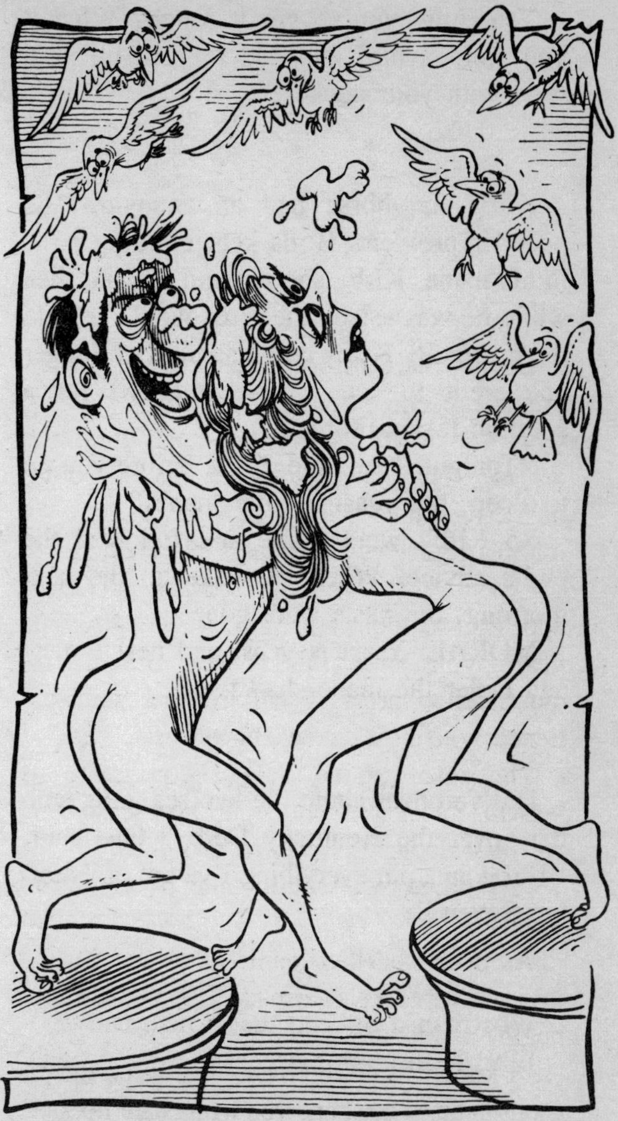

You think you've got it rough? What if you were a bird and had to pick up your food with your pecker?

*   *   *

Kirby the horse had an annoying and peculiar problem: Birds kept building nests in his mane. Kirby shook them off, but then while he was asleep the birds would rebuild them. Finally Kirby could stand it no longer and went to see a wise old owl for a solution to his problem.

"Tonight," said the owl, "before you go to sleep, put yeast in your mane."

So Kirby went home and followed the owl's advice. When he woke up the next morning, the nests were gone.

MORAL: Yeast is yeast and nest is nest and never the mane shall tweet.

*   *   *

Did you hear about the two sea gulls who flew over the Kentucky Derby? One said, "I'm gonna put everything I've got on Number Seven."

*   *   *

What can a bird do that a man can't? Whistle through his pecker.

*   *   *

Perry Bingham, the dynamic Santa Rosa dentist, doubles up patients with this doozy:

Doctor Upton was visiting a mental institution. Walking around the grounds, he noticed an inmate perched on a branch of a tree.

"Who are you?" asked the M.D.

"Tweet, tweet," replied the inmate. "One beautiful spring evening my father and mother went for a lark, and I'm the lark—tweet, tweet."

* * *

It's a queer termite that goes for a woodpecker.

* * *

Here's to the stork,
A most valuable bird
That inhabits the residential districts.
He doesn't sing tunes
Nor yield any plumes,
But he helps out the vital statistics.

* * *

Did you hear about the birdhouse that was named HOME TWEET HOME?

* * *

The Marlins owned a Rary bird, an uncommon and very unusual species. They took extra care of this Rary bird because they loved it so much. One summer the couple decided to visit Montreal for a vacation. They left enough food for the Rary bird to eat while they were gone.

When they returned two weeks later, the Rary bird had eaten all the drapes, the rugs, the furniture. Mrs. Marlin became hysterical and ordered her husband to take the bird out and drop him off a cliff. Marlin took the bird, climbed a steep hill, and placed it on the edge of the cliff. He was just about to push it over when the Rary bird, looked down, then up at Marlin and said, "That's a long way to tip a Rary!"

*   *   *

Max and Humphrey, two eagles, were lazily soaring over the desert when a jet plane sped by them, its exhaust spouting flame and smoke. As it went out of sight, Max remarked, "That bird was really in a hurry."

"You'd be in a hurry too," said Humphrey, "if your tail was on fire."

*   *   *

What's grey?
A melted penguin.

*   *   *

"Hey, Harlow, why so glum?"
"I spotted the first robin of spring."
"What's so bad about that?"
"He spotted me first."

* * *

In the park, someone who was having lunch was not hungry enough to finish his bologna sandwiches so he threw a piece of bologna to the birds.

One blue jay ate the bologna and it started to sing for joy. This attracted the attention of a nasty cat who pounced and terminated the bird's life.

MORAL: Never open your mouth when you are full of bologna!

* * *

Wendell, the amorous eagle, in quest of a mate, seized a dove and carried it to his cave. Once in the nest, he made love to her. While leaving, she sang, "I'm a dove! I'm a dove! I love to love!"

Then the eagle caught a loon. In the nest his captive crooned, "I'm a loon! I'm a loon! I love to spoon!"

Then the eagle captured a duck. But in the nest, the duck quacked, "I'm a drake! I'm a drake! Oy! Have you made a mistake!"

* * *

"Do you have any birdseed?"

"What kind of bird do you have?"

"I don't have a bird. I want to grow one."

* * *

Why are there more sparrows than squirrels?

Because screwing in the trees is for the birds!

* * *

An ornithologist is troubled by the fact that the stork is too often held responsible for circumstances that might better be attributed to a lark.

* * *

Did you hear about the bird that goes "Oooh! Ahh! Ooh! Ahh!?"

The bird weighs four and a half pounds and it lays an egg that weighs two and a half pounds. And as she lays the egg she goes "Oooh Ahh!"

* * *

Then there was the romantic young firefly who could hardly wait to glow up.

* * *

Farmer Wilkins, on his way to doing chores one cold wintry day, saw a bird freezing in a field. He couldn't take the bird with him and he knew if he left it, the bird would freeze to death.

Wilkins saw a pile of fresh, warm horse manure. So he picked up the bird and put it in the manure so it wouldn't freeze and went on to get his work done.

The bird slowly but surely began to thaw out and pretty soon began to chirp. Suddenly, a cat that was passing, heard the chirping, ran over to the pile of manure, grabbed the bird and ate him.

There are three morals to this story:

1. A person who puts you into a pile of manure—is not necessarily bad.
2. Someone who takes you out of the pile—is not necessarily good.
3. When you're warm and comfortable—even if it's in a pile of manure—keep your mouth shut!

Farm Fables

While walking along a back road, Dalton noticed a farmer driving a horse which every now and then stopped suddenly and then started again only with difficulty.

"What's the matter? Is your horse sick?" inquired the pedestrian.

"No," replied the farmer.

"Balky?" continued Dalton.

"No," explained the farmer. "This horse is so worried I'll say 'whoa' and he won't hear me, that he stops every once in a while to listen."

*   *   *

Coreen, the glamorous cow, was leisurely grazing in a lush patch of green. On one side of the pasture she discovered a barbed-wire fence that was eight feet tall. But on the other side of this fence was the handsomest bull Coreen had ever laid eyes on. She and the bull began to flirt. "You must come over and see me sometime," said Coreen, "if you think you can jump that fence." And she flicked her tail and walked away.

Taunted by the invitation, the bull backed up. Lowered his head, took a long run, jumped over the fence, and landed beside Coreen.

"Say. I know you," exclaimed Coreen. "You're Baldwin the bull."

"Just call me Baldy," said the bull, "that fence was higher than I thought it was."

*　　*　　*

What goes "Nort, Nort?"
A bull with a cleft palate.

* * *

What do you call a cow with no legs?
Ground beef.

* * *

Did you hear about the farmer who had a real muscular bull on his farm?
He put him on a diet so he could get into a tight jersey.

* * *

And what about the cow that got a divorce because she got a bum steer?

* * *

Clem, a young farmboy, head hung in submission, sat across from a priest in the church confessional. "Forgive me, Father, for I have sinned," he admitted. "I been havin' sex with some of the animals on our farm."

"Hmm," muttered the priest. "Were these animals male or female?"

"What the hell do you think I am," shouted Clem, "a fairy?"

* * *

Jillson, an Indiana farmer, telephoned the vet.

"What's the trouble?" asked the doctor.

"It's my prize bull. It's time for him to get together with the cows, but the critter won't make a move. You better come over and see what's ailing him."

The vet arrived with a bagful of hormones, vitamins, and special pills, went into the barn, and worked on the bull for half an hour.

"I took care of him," he said. "By tomorrow afternoon he'll be back in peak condition."

Several days later, Jillson called the vet again. "Now what's wrong?" asked the animal doctor.

"Last night I put my bull in the barn with two cows—and not a dangblasted thing happened!"

"What did you expect? To have a calf overnight?" asked the vet.

"Hell no! But at least I expected to see two happy faces!"

* * *

What do you get when you cross a tortoise with a cow?

A turtleneck jersey.

* * *

Seen the porno movie about animal sodomy?

It's called Sheep Throat.

Caldwell was returning from a duck-hunting trip with an empty bag when he saw some ducks in a pond. Nearby, Peabody was leaning on a fence watching them.

"What'll you take for letting me have a shot at those ducks?" asked Caldwell.

"Oh," said Peabody, "I'll take ten dollars."

"Okay," said the hunter. Caldwell fired into the middle of the flock, killing about a dozen. "I'm afraid you made a bad bargain," he added.

"I don't know," said Peabody. "They're not my ducks."

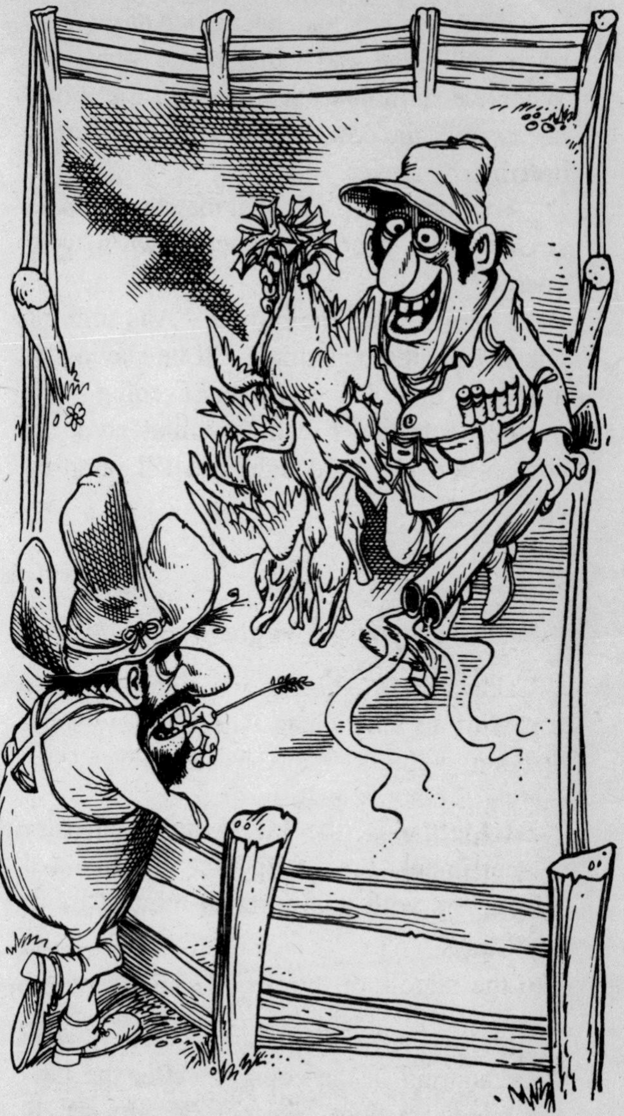

Farmer Dewitt had been to Kansas City on a big binge and came home very late. When he stumbled out at five in the morning to milk the cow, he was suffering from a horrible hangover.

"You look terrible," said the cow. "Those circles under your eyes reach down to your knees."

"I know," said the farmer. "And milking you is only the beginning. I'll be slaving on this durn farm 'til seven this evening."

"I'll help all I can," volunteered the cow. "You just hold tight and I'll jump up and down."

*   *   *

Where do you get virgin wool?
From ugly sheep.

*   *   *

Ed McManus, the Massachusetts master of merriment, breaks up his "Jokesmith" subscribers with this mirthful mint of monkeyshines:

Bigelow, a New England attorney, went duck hunting in the country. After the lawyer bagged a duck, Farmer Ferraro caught him and cried, "You're on private property and that duck is mine."

"Ridiculous!" said Bigelow. "I shot that while it was flying and people don't own air rights over property. I shot it, I picked it up, I own it."

"Mister," said Ferraro, "out here we settle property disputes the old-fashioned way."

"How's that?" asked the lawyer.

"First, I kick you in the groin," said the farmer, "then you kick me same place. We do that till one of us gives up."

Bigelow had on heavy hunting boots. He noticed the farmer wearing rubber boots and so he agreed.

Ferraro took a running start, thrust out his leg, and kicked the lawyer in the groin with all his might. Bigelow dropped to the ground in agony.

Fifteen minutes later the lawyer gasped, "Now it's my turn!"

"No," said the farmer, "Keep it. I give up!"

*　　*　　*

QUACK

A perfect pwace to put a pwick.

*　　*　　*

Old Doc Dannon was packing up his little black bag after examining Farmer Bradford. He turned to him and said, "Bradford, I'm not coming out to see you anymore."

"What's the matter, Doctor?"

"Why, everytime I visit you, your ducks insult me."

*   *   *

Why can't a baby duck lay eggs?
The quack's too small.

*   *   *

New Yorker: Look at that bunch of cows.
Farmer: Not bunch . . . herd.
New Yorker: Heard what?
Farmer: Herd of cows.
New Yorker: Sure I've heard of cows.
Farmer: No, a cow herd.
New Yorker: Why should I care what a cow heard? I've got no secrets from a cow.

*   *   *

The Ohio State coed asked an old farmer: "Which is correct grammatically, sir, to say a hen is 'setting' or 'sitting'?"

"I don't know, miss," replied the farmer, "and it don't interest me none. What I wonder, when I hear a hen cackle, is if she's 'laying' or 'lying.'"

* * *

"That was a terrible storm you had down your way, Willard."

"Sure was. Our hen had her back to the wind and she laid the same egg five times."

* * *

The Alabama preacher was loudly condemning human stupidity in putting vile alcohol in the stomach.

"Suppose," he raved, "I set a pail of water and a pail of beer before a donkey. Which would he drink?"

"The water," cried Farmer Colby from the rear.

"Exactly," thundered the preacher. "And why would the creature drink the water?"

"Because he's an ass," declared the farmer.

* * *

A county fair in Wisconsin brought folks from far and wide. Farmer Johanson from the southern part of the state attended the fair especially because he wanted to see the grand prize champion bull. And he brought his whole family. When Johanson arrived at the entrance, he found that he and his wife and three eldest children would have to pay five dollars each and the other eight children three dollars. Being a cattle-minded man, he kicked like a steer. The manager walked by and asked, "What's the problem?"

"Well," said the farmer, "me and the wife and the children have traveled more'n two hundred miles to see that champion bull, but I'll be danged if I can afford to pay forty-nine dollars to get in."

"Are all these children yours?" asked the manager.

"They certainly are," said Johanson.

The manager said to the cashier, "Let 'em in free."

Then he said to the farmer, "We want that bull to see you."

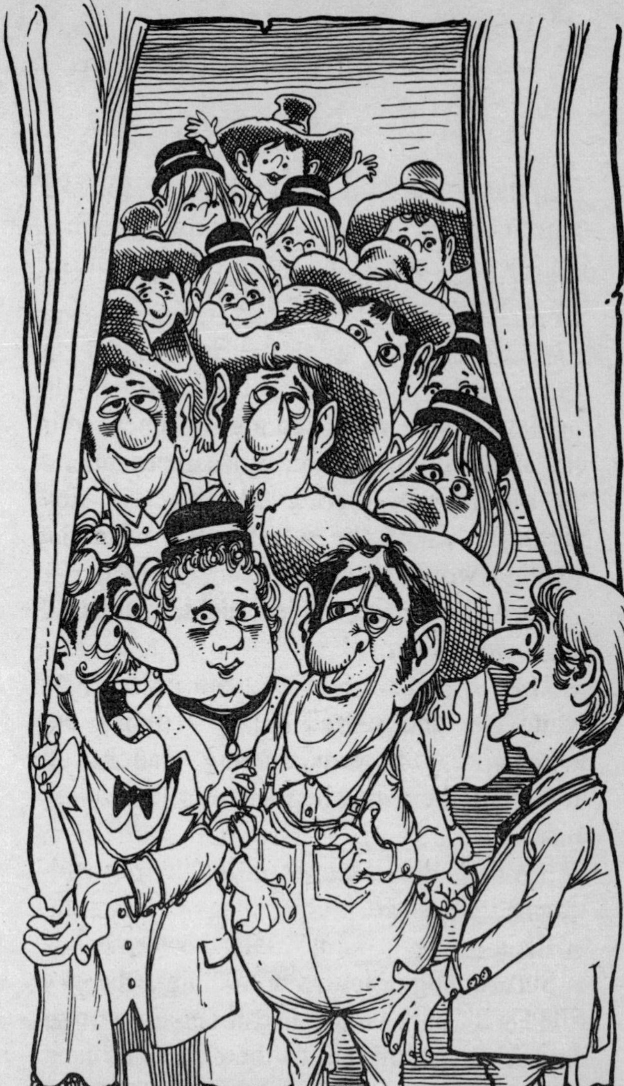

"Why do ducks dive?"

"Guess they want to liquidate their bills."

*   *   *

In the pond out in the back of a Nebraska barn, a couple of frogs were jumping around. Finally one said to the other, "Time sure is fun when you're having flies!"

*   *   *

Many, many years ago a government official in Washington hired a weatherman. As the official was leaving the office the first night, he asked the weatherman what the weather would be.

"It will be a bright, clear night," predicted the weatherman.

That evening the official put on his new white suit and started out to a dinner engagement. As he walked along, glancing up at the cloudless sky, he met a farmer leading a donkey.

"What's the weather going to be, old-timer?" he asked.

"It's going to rain," said the farmer.

Sure enough, ten minutes later, the sky filled with dark clouds and it began to pour, drenching the official to the skin. The next day he looked up the farmer.

"I want to hire you as a weatherman," he told him.

"It ain't me," said the farmer. "It's my donkey." "Everytime that critter's ears hang down, it's sure to rain."

"Okay," said the official, "then I'll hire the donkey."

And he did. And that's why ever since, there have been jackasses in Washington.

*   *   *

"My," said the Boston girl, "what a strange-looking cow. Why doesn't she have any horns?"

"There're lots of reasons cows don't have horns," explained the farmer. "Some we de-horn, and some are born without horns, and some shed their horns. But there's a simple reason why *that* cow hasn't got horns. It's a mule."

*   *   *

There was a Maine farmer named Morse
Who fell madly in love with his horse.
 Said his wife, "You rapscallion,
 That horse is a stallion—
This constitutes grounds for divorce."

*   *   *

111

Why do frogs have the shortest sex life in the animal kingdom?

They hop on, hop off . . . and then croak.

* * *

Zacariah decided to make some money off his pet stallion Rusty at the county fair. The farmer offered a hundred dollars to anyone who could make the animal laugh.

Each contestant paid Zacariah five dollars. They stood in front of Rusty and made funny faces, some did tricks, a few even told jokes, but the horse didn't crack a smile. By the end of the day, Zacariah cleaned up two hundred dollars.

Then Feinberg, a little old man, paid Zacariah the five dollars, climbed on a stool, cupped his hand and whispered in the animal's ear. Rusty broke into mirthful neighing and whinnying. Zacariah handed over the hundred dollars.

Next day Zacariah offered a hundred dollars to anyone who could make Rusty cry. Everybody tried but by day's end, the farmer had recouped the money he had lost. Just then Feinberg showed up and dropped his pants in front of the stallion. Rusty began to weep uncontrollably.

Hitching up his pants, Feinberg collected his money and started away.

"Wait a minute!" shouted the farmer. "What made my horse act like that?"

"Yesterday, I told him my penis was bigger than his. Today, I showed him."

Zoo Zanies

It was a world-famous zoo. The animals had been collected from the four corners of the earth and they were allowed to roam freely about the grounds.

A hippopotamus stood next to a giraffe. The giraffe peered over the fence and said to the hippo, "Boy, I sure feel lousy. I have a sore throat. It's killing me!"

"You think you've got troubles!" exclaimed the hippo. "I have chapped lips!"

* * *

"Is that a man-eating lion?"

"Yes, lady, but we're short of men this week, so all he gets is beef."

* * *

Little Todd and his slightly deaf grandfather were at the San Diego Zoo watching the laughing hyenas. An attendant told the crowd that the hyena ate forty-three pounds of meat a week. Grandpa leaned over to his grandson and asked, "What'd he say?"

Todd repeated the fellow's remarks into his granddaddy's ear.

"The laughing hyena," continued the attendant, "is unusual because after digesting all that food, he usually evacuates only once a month." Again Grandpa asked, "What'd he say?"

The boy told him.

"Sonny," crowed the old man, "if that damn thing eats forty-three pounds of meat a week and has only one bowel movement a month, what the hell is he laughing about?"

*   *   *

What must a lion tamer know to teach a lion tricks?

More than the lion.

*   *   *

What do Tupperware and a walrus have in common?

They both like a tight seal.

*   *   *

Karen Warner, the witty California comedy scribe, wows buddies with this snippet of silly satire:

The new lion in the zoo was fed a few bananas while the old lion in the next cage was given big chunks of raw meat. The new lion finally asked the older one, "How come I get only bananas while you get steak?"

"This zoo," explained the old lion, "works on a low budget, and they've got you registered as a monkey."

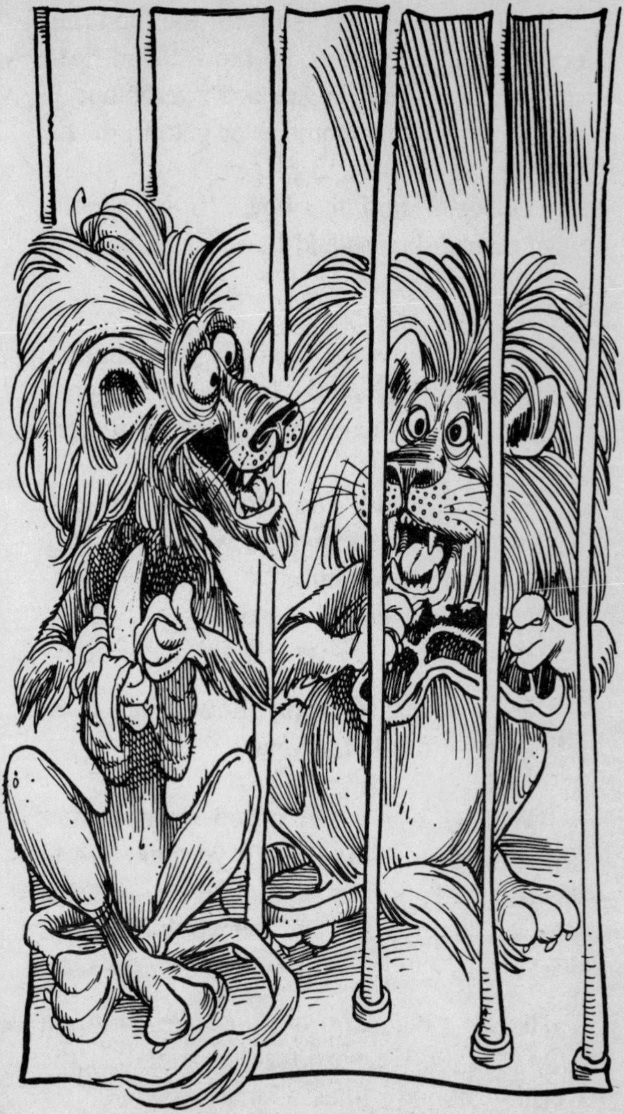

Baldwin took his son to the zoo and pointed out the lions to him. "Son," he cautioned, "there is the most ferocious of all animals. If he should ever get out of that cage, he'd tear me to pieces."

"Daddy," said the boy, "if he should, what number bus should I take to get home?"

*   *   *

Johnson, his wife, and his two children were visiting the zoo. They finally stopped in front of the cage of a large, ferocious lion.

"Honey," said Mrs. Johnson, "if that lion were to escape, whom would you save first, me or the children?"

"Me," answered Johnson.

*   *   *

Here's a classic Jerry Lewis has been telling on himself for years:

"When I was a kid I said to my father one afternoon, 'Daddy, will you take me to the zoo?' My father said, 'If the zoo wants you, let them come and get you!'"

*   *   *

The St. Louis Zoo has a donkey with an I.Q. of 150. He hasn't got a friend in the world— nobody likes a smart ass!

*   *   *

The zoo keeper found a new employee standing uneasily before the lion's cage.

Keeper: Didn't I tell you when a lion wagged his tail, he was friendly?

Employee: Yeah, but he was wagging his tail and roaring at the same time.

Keeper: Well, what's that got to do with it?

Employee: I didn't know which end to believe.

* * *

The eminent Mrs. Larue
Was born in a cage at the zoo
   And the curious rape
   Which made her an ape
Is highly fantastic, if true.

* * *

Hamilton was playing "Monkey See, Monkey Do" with one of the zoo gorillas. He showed it how to stick out its tongue, snap its fingers and got excellent responses. But when Hamilton rubbed his eye with one hand the gorilla went berserk, pulling open its cage and almost killing the poor fellow.

Later, a zoo attendant explained to Hamilton that rubbing your eye means "Up yours" in gorilla language.

When Hamilton was released from the hospital, he went to a deli, bought a big roll of bologna, stuck it in his pants, and went back to the gorilla cage. Hamilton pulled it part way out, whacked it off with his pocket knife, then handed the knife to the anthropoid.

The gorilla rubbed an eye at him. . . .

ZOO

A place where strong cages are used to protect the animals from the public.

Furry Funnies

"And here's a little pet I've brought from Central America to remind you of me."

"Oh, Will, how kind of you to bring me this dear little monkey. It is just like you."

* * *

The Wilkinson family was picnicking in the country. The children had been playing in the fields when little Karla rushed up to her mother and exclaimed, "Mother, Rickey wants the mouthwash, quick. He just caught the cutest little black and white animal and he thinks it's got bad breath."

* * *

Imelda had two pet monkeys. One of them died suddenly. The other immediately took sick, refused to eat, and died of a broken heart. Imelda felt very bad and, wishing to preserve them, brought them to a taxidermist.

"Do you want to have these monkeys mounted?" asked the taxidermist.

"Oh, no," she replied. "Just have them holding hands."

*   *   *

The organ-grinder and his monkey had amused the children immensely. They had all dropped their pennies in the monkey's cap when he had come around to beg. Later, Anabel told her mother about the monkey's antics.

"What did the monkey do with the pennies?" asked her mother.

"He gave them to his father," said the child.

*   *   *

"I spotted a leopard yesterday."

"You can't fool me. They grow that way."

*   *   *

Turtle, Buzzard, and Rabbit were schoolmates. When they got out on their own, Turtle and Buzzard prospered and became wealthy. They shared a large estate together and became very uppity.

Rabbit was in the fertilizer business. He received an order from Turtle and Buzzard and went to deliver the fertilizer. He was met at the door by a snooty uniformed butler.

"I want to see Mr. Turtle or Mr. Buzzard," stated Rabbit.

"Oh," said the stuffy English butler, "Mr. Tur-*til* is over the hill and Mr. Buz-*zard* is out in the yard."

"Well," answered Rabbit, "will you tell Mr. Tur-*til,* who is over the hill, or Mr. Buz-*zard,* who is out in the yard, that Mr. Rab-*bit* is here with the shit!"

*   *   *

Three rabbits were arrested on a charge of vagrancy and brought to court. Judge Jorgenson asked the first rabbit: "What's your name and your occupation?"

"I'm Jack Rabbit," he replied. "I pick up pebbles on the beach."

"And what's your name?" inquired Jorgenson of the second rabbit.

"I'm Brer Rabbit," he said. "I help him pick up pebbles."

The judge turned to the third rabbit and asked, "And what have you to say for yourself?"

"I'm Pebbles," she answered.

*   *   *

Russ Root, Gualala's popular tale-teller, gets roars with this rib-tickler:

The San Quentin chaplin, on a tour of inspection one day, noticed an inmate feeding a rat.

"I see," he said, "you have a pet."

"Yes, sir," replied the prisoner. "This rat is a real pet. I feed him every day. I think more of him than I do any other living creature."

"I am glad to hear that," said the chaplin. "In every human being there is something of the angel, if we can only find it. How did you happen to make a pet of this rat?"

"He bit the guard," answered the prisoner.

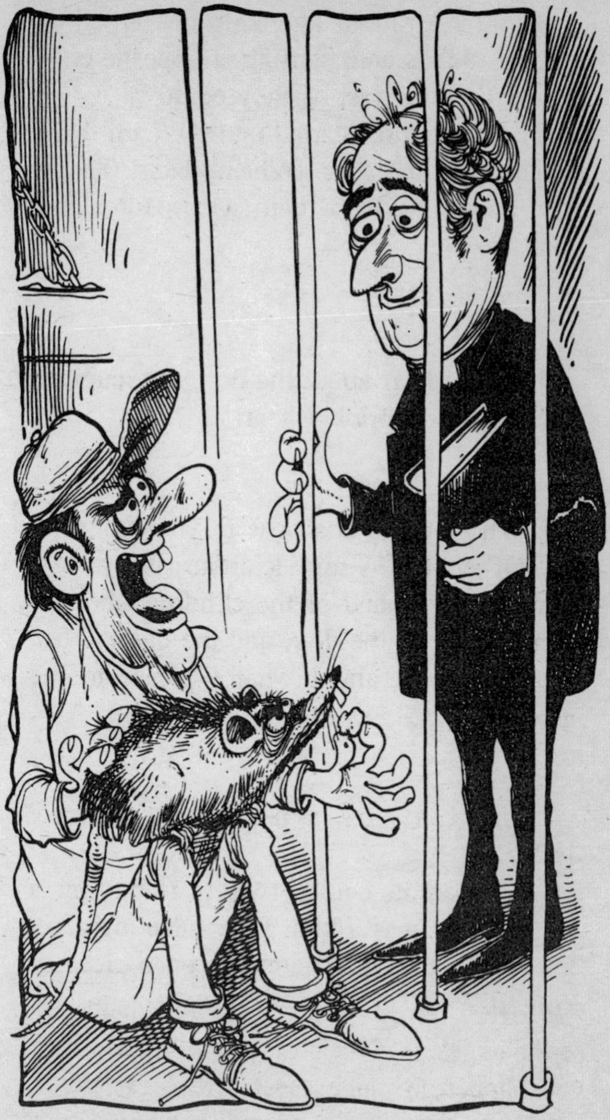

Two buck rabbits agreed to line up all the female rabbits and, starting at opposite ends, screw them as fast as they could.

The first rabbit started out: "Wham, bam! Thank you ma'am!—Wham, bam! Thank-you ma'am! Wham, bam! Oh, pardon me, Sam."

* * *

Did you hear about the horny porcupine? She was in prickly heat!

* * *

"Who's really the boss in your house?"

"Of course," said Riordan, "my wife assumes command of the children, the servants, the cat, the dog, and the canary. But I can say just about what I please to the goldfish."

* * *

"Did you have a pet when you were little?"

"My parents couldn't afford to buy me a dog when I was a kid. They gave me a pet ant. I had to paper-train him on a piece of confetti."

* * *

Conway and Darlene, two lovers, were deeply interested in reincarnation. They even vowed that if either died, the one remaining would try to contact the partner in the other world exactly thirty days after the tragedy.

A few weeks later, Conway died suddenly, and Darlene attempted to contact him in the spirit world thirty days later. "Conway, darling," she cried, "this is Darlene. Do you hear me, lover?"

"Yes, Darlene," answered a ghostly voice. "I hear you."

"Oh, Conway, what's it like where you are?"

"It's beautiful. There are azure skies, soft breezes, and quiet prairies sweeping the horizon."

"It sounds beautiful. What do you do all day?"

"We're all up before sunrise, eat breakfast, and then it's nothing but sex until noon. After lunch, we nap 'til two and then make love until five. After dinner there's more of the same 'til midnight, when we go to sleep to get ready for the next morning."

"But, Conway, is that really what heaven is like?"

"Heaven? I'm not in heaven. I'm a jackrabbit in Wyoming!"

* * *

Young Chip swore a lot. His parents tried to get him to stop, but without success. One day his father said, "Chip, you've always wanted a rabbit, and if you promise not to swear anymore, I'll get you one."

"Okay, Dad. I promise."

Chip got his rabbit and for two weeks, he stuck to his bargain. One day Uncle Milton came to the house, and said, "I hear you've got a rabbit. Wouldn't you like to show it to me?"

The boy rushed out to the garden to collect his pet. Just as he brought it into the living room that rabbit began giving birth to an enormous litter of baby rabbits. Chip dropped the mother rabbit and cried, "Holy Christ, the goddamned thing is falling apart."

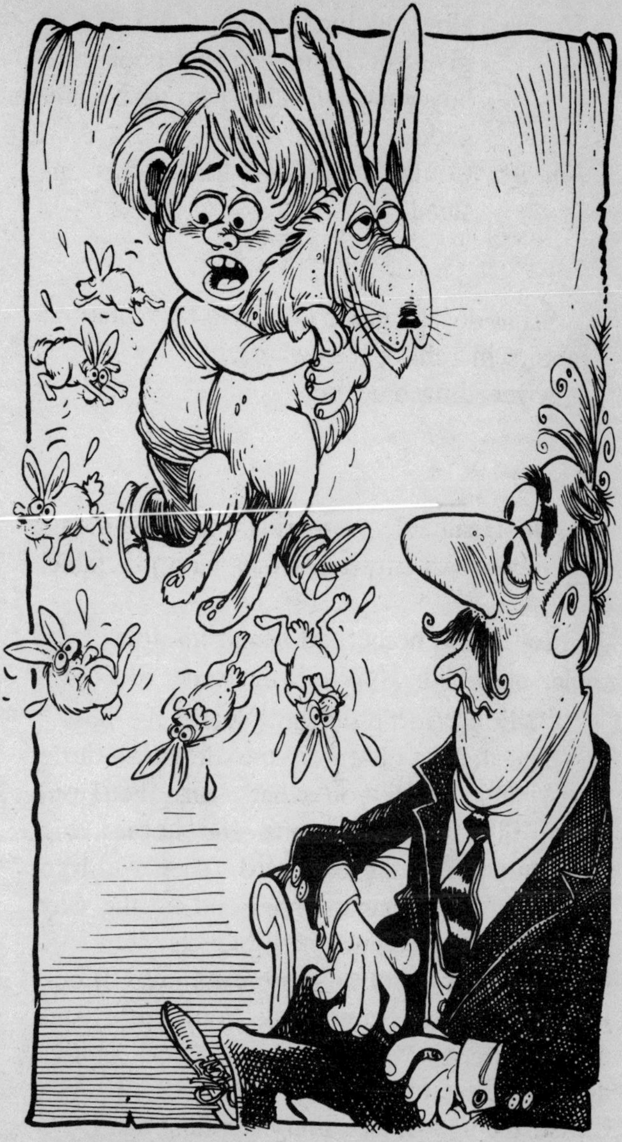

Mother: Now, Junior, wouldn't you like to give your bunny to that poor little boy you saw today who hasn't any daddy?

Junior: Couldn't we give him Father instead?

*　　*　　*

What do you get if you have five hundred rabbits marching backwards in a row?

A receding hare line.

*　　*　　*

Dr. Dean Edel, America's favorite media medicine man, fractures fans with this fable:

Jeff came home and found his four-year-old son sobbing. "What's the matter, Bobby?"

"My pet turtle's dead!" cried the boy.

The father observed the dormant turtle and said, "Tell you what, son. We'll put him in a nice little box and have a big funeral out in the backyard. Then we'll go get you a big banana split and on the way home I'll buy you a new bicycle."

Just then the turtle began to move. "Look son, isn't that wonderful. Your turtle isn't dead after all!"

"Daddy! Let's kill it!"

*　　*　　*

Papa Rabbit noticed with some interest that his young son was looking uncommonly contented with life. "What makes Junior so happy?" he asked Mama Rabbit when they were alone.

"He had a great day in school," she explained. "He learned to multiply."

*   *   *

Little squirrel with your pants so low
What makes you walk so slow
Pull up your pants, increase your stride
Little squirrel you has nuts to hide.

*   *   *

Rabbits have such funny faces,
Their private lives are such disgraces,
   You'd be surprised if you but knew
   The awful things that rabbits do
And often, too.

*   *   *

Marion and boyfriend Wes were sitting on a blanket in the country. A bug lit on her cap and she exclaimed, "Oh, look at this funny little bug. What kind is it?"

"That's a ladybug," he replied.

"My, but you have good eyesight."

*   *   *

What do you call a rabbit with herpes?
Peter Rotten Tail.

PET LOVERS LAMENT

Mary's lamb I quite despise,
Her tastes in pets astound me.
But Mary's calves . . .
Now there's a pair
I'd love to have around me.

* * *

Two dogs were chasing two rabbits, when one rabbit turned to the other and said, "Let's stop here for a few minutes and outnumber them."

* * *

What would you call a rabbit with the crabs?
Bugs Bunny!

* * *

What does the little mouse do with his tail when he goes to bed?
He enjoys it.

* * *

Said Mrs. Rabbit
To Mr. Rabbit:
"Sex is just a habit."
Said Mr. Rabbit
To Mrs. Rabbit:
"Slip the habit to me, Rabbit."

* * *

What did one little mouse say to the other?

"Come over in the corner and I'll show you my hole!"

* * *

Why do you want a divorce?" the judge asked Cantrell.

"My wife insists upon keeping a pet goat in the bedroom," he explained. "The smell is so bad I can't stand it any longer."

"Well," questioned the judge, "have you tried to open the window?"

"What?" cried the husband. "And let all my pigeons out?"

* * *

"I bought a goat this morning."

"Where are you going to keep it?"

"In the house."

"But what about the smell?"

"The goat won't mind."

* * *

At their annual football game, the big animals were trouncing the little animals with a tremendous offensive game. At halftime the score was 42-0. The little animals kicked off and managed to stop the opposition on the twenty-two-yard line. On first down, the big animals sent the hippopotamus around right end, but he was stopped cold at the line of scrimmage.

Back in the huddle, the squirrel, captain of the little animals, said, "Hey, that was great! Who stopped the hippo, anyway?"

"Me," said the centipede.

On second down, the rhino charged around left end, but was stopped for a two-yard loss. "Terrific," cheered the squirrel. "Who did it this time?"

"Me," said the centipede.

On third down, the big animals sent the elephant up the middle, but he was knocked flat on his back. "Was that you again?" the squirrel asked the bug.

"Yup," said the centipede.

"Where the hell were you during the first half?" demanded the captain.

"Taping my ankles."

Tale Waggery

Heidi and Bon Bon, two prize-winning Pekingese, were passing the time of day.

"I'm very nervous right now. Can't face a dog biscuit," confided Heidi. "And I'm not sleeping well, I get spots before my eyes, I'm terrified of cats—"

"Listen," said Bon Bon, "maybe you should go see a psychiatrist."

"That wouldn't work," sighed Heidi, "I'm not allowed on the couch."

*   *   *

Every boy who has a dog should also have a mother, so the dog can be fed regularly.

*   *   *

Why is dog man's best friend?

It doesn't give advice, never tries to borrow money, and has no in-laws.

*   *   *

Little Richard's dog Paddy had been run over by a car and the boy's mother felt awful about breaking the news to him. When the youngster came home from school he said, "Where's Paddy?"

His mother said, "Paddy's been killed by an automobile."

Richard said, "Oh?" and left the house whistling.

That night at dinner the boy said, "Hey, Mom, where's Paddy?"

She said, "Darling, I told you this afternoon that Paddy was killed by a car."

Richard began crying. His mother said, "When I told you this afternoon, it didn't seem to bother you."

"I thought you said Daddy!"

*   *   *

A blind man with a guide dog entered a Philadelphia department store. He stopped, picked up his dog by the tail, and began swinging the animal over his head. A clerk hurried over and asked, "May I help you?"

"No thanks," said the blind man. "I'm just looking around."

*   *   *

"Our dog is just like one of the family."
"Really? Which one?"

* * *

When Kenneth was a little boy, he took fiddle lessons. One day while he was practicing, scraping dismally back and forth with his bow, his dog sent up a plaintive wailing and howling. Finally his sister Flossie, who was trying to do her homework, stuck her head into the room where her brother was practicing.

"For goodness sake!" she complained. "Can't you play something the dog doesn't know?"

* * *

DOGMA

A puppy's mother.

* * *

"Your husband says he leads a dog's life."
"Yes, it's very similar. He comes in with muddy feet, makes himself comfortable by the fire, and waits to be fed."

* * *

Bob Heffernan, Santa Rosa's top printer, gets chuckles from this choice bit of chicanery:

Chadwell went to visit his friend Monson and was amazed to find him playing chess with his dog. Chadwell watched the game in pop-eyed astonishment for a while.

"I can hardly believe my eyes," he exclaimed. "That's the smartest dog I've ever seen."

"Aw, he's not so smart," replied Monson. "I've beaten him three games out of five."

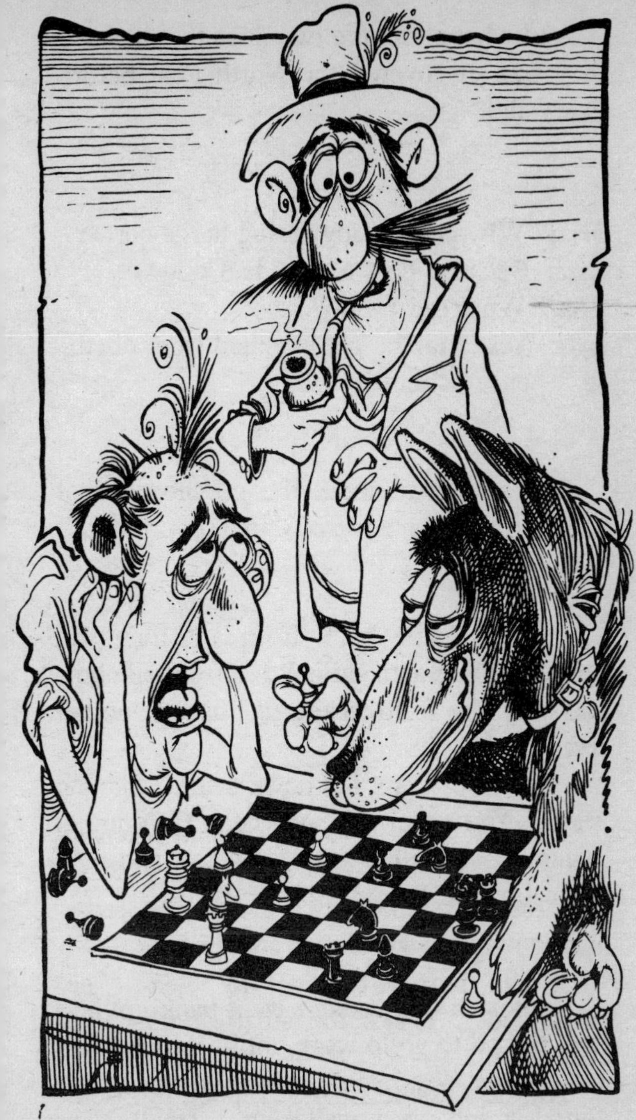

And what about the two dogs that insisted they had discovered the North Pole before Peary did.

*   *   *

Fred: Why is your dog sitting in the corner?
Lyle: Because he's a very bad doggie.
Fred: What did he do?
Lyle: Yesterday he got expelled from obedience school.

*   *   *

Did you hear about the greyhound that ran so fast he made sixty trees an hour?

*   *   *

Furman came back from a selling trip through the South during July. "Well, how did you like it down there?" asked another sales rep.

"Oh, boy, was it hot down there," Furman said. "You never felt such heat. One day in Atlanta I saw a dog chasing a cat, and they were both walking."

*   *   *

Denton, a dog trainer, went bankrupt and was forced to go to work until he could start out in the dog-raising business again. He found a job as a waiter in a small New Orleans restaurant. After working for a few days, Denton said to the owner of the place, "I'm turning out to be a pretty good waiter, don't you think?"

Said the proprietor, "If you don't mind, I'm going to make a couple of suggestions about your work."

"Such as?" asked Denton.

"Well," said the owner, "when the customer refuses to eat his food, we don't rub his nose in it!"

*   *   *

Did you hear about the chef who gave his dog some garlic and now his bark is worse than his bite?

*   *   *

Then there's the guy whose dog had large cauliflower ears, but he said it was normal. His dog was a boxer.

*   *   *

"What is it about a dachshund that you don't care for?"

"They make such a draft when they come into a room. They always keep the door open so long."

*   *   *

DACHSHUND

A dog-and-a-half long
And a half a dog high

*   *   *

It was past midnight when the telephone rang in the veterinarian's home. "Shay, are you a dog doctor?" slobbered a drunken voice.

"Yes," replied the doc.

"If I come over will you bark for me?"

* * *

"Lay down, pup," said the visitor. "Come on, doggie, lay down. That's a good doggie. For heaven's sake—lay down, will you?"

"S'cuse me," said the host, "but you'll have to say 'lie down.' He's a Boston terrier."

* * *

It was a terrible night. The rain was coming down in sheets. The wind was blowing fiercely and visibility was almost nil. Whittaker, the farm machinery salesman, was driving through the back roads of Missouri.

"This is a rough one," he told his pet dog, who accompanied him on all his trips. "Looks like we're in for it!"

Whittaker spotted a small motel. He picked up his pup, ran in, and said to the desk clerk, "I'd like a room for tonight."

142

"Sorry, mister," said the redneck clerk, "we're all filled up."

"I could sleep on the sofa," suggested the salesman.

"That's where ah sleep."

"But you can't turn me out on a night like this," protested Whittaker. "It's pouring rain."

The clerk shrugged. The salesman realized it was useless to plead. He turned to go, but the clerk said, "Just a minute, mister. Leave the pup here. Ah wouldn't turn a dog out on a night like this!"

* * *

SIGN IN A PET SHOP WINDOW:
Buy your dog a new leash on life.

* * *

"My dog is the smartest canine in the world," bragged Appleton.

"Really?" said Halley.

"Last month, when our house caught on fire, we all got out safely, but my dog dashed back inside through the smoke and flames. And what do you suppose he brought back out in his mouth?"

"What?" asked Appleton.

"Our insurance policy, wrapped up in a damp towel."

* * *

Jeannine Riley, the ravishing redheaded TV actress, gets roars with this rib-buster:

Three-year-old Candace loved dogs. One day while she was playing out in front of her house she saw a huge boxer down the street and ran toward him, shouting, "Hi, doggie! Hi, doggie!"

The big dog bounded to her and stopped just when they were nose to nose. Candace gazed up at him and said, "Hi, horsey!"

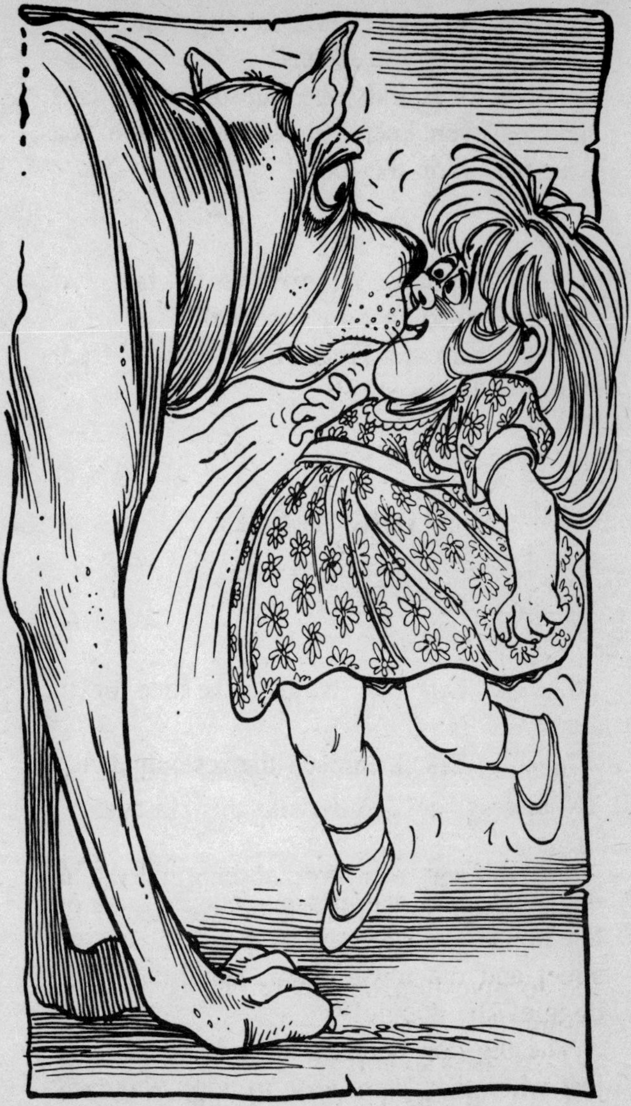

"My new dog is very thoughtful."

"What do you mean?"

"He loves kids, he doesn't chase cars, and he even keeps his tail up so the fleas can play loop-the-loop."

* * *

"Your puppy is growing so fast, you must be feeding him very well."

"We sure are. He ate three pairs of Dad's slippers last week."

* * *

DOG KENNEL

Chock Full O' Mutts.

* * *

Hostess: Our dog is just like one of the family.

Guest: Yes, I can see the resemblance.

* * *

Kevin was the most absentminded altar boy Father O'Malley had ever seen. But Kevin meant well, and the clergyman decided to give him one more chance to prove himself.

"At mass tomorrow you'll hear me sing, 'And God's angels lit the candles.' When I

146

say that, you light the candles in the back of the church. Is that understood?''

''Yes, Father,'' said the boy.

Next day the priest conducted mass in front of a full congregation. At last his rich tenor sang out, ''And God's angels lit the candles!''

Nothing happened. Again he intoned, ''And God's angels lit the candles!''

Still the candles remained unlit. Once more he boomed, ''And God's angels lit the candles!''

From behind the last pew Kevin cried out, ''And your dog pissed on the matches!''

* * *

Did you hear about the dog that visited a flea circus and stole the show?

* * *

The only two who can live as cheaply as one are a dog and a flea.

* * *

What did one flea say to the other flea when they wanted to get across town?

''Should we walk or should we take a dog?''

* * *

"How do you get rid of a dog's fleas?"

"Give him a bath in alcohol and a rub-down with sand. The fleas get drunk and kill each other throwing rocks."

* * *

Aunt Louise: I'm going to enter Mitzi in the dog show next month.

Auntie Ag: Do you think she'll win many prizes?

Aunt Louise: No, but she'll meet some very nice dogs.

* * *

A wealthy Beverly Hills Iranian had a dog who had his own little doghouse complete with little furniture. A neighbor was looking at it one day and asked, "How does he keep it so clean?"

"Oh," said the Iranian, "he has a Mexican chihuahua come in once a week."

* * *

The big 767 jet landed in Atlanta. As the baggage handlers removed a pet carrier they were shocked to discover the little wirehaired terrier inside was dead.

The airline, fearful of being sued, scoured the city to find a dog that looked exactly like the dead canine. By that afternoon they finally found one and sent their marketing director out to the owner's home.

He proudly presented a beautiful barking wirehaired terrier to the woman. She stood in the doorway in stony silence.

"Is there anything wrong?" asked the airline director.

"That isn't my dog!" snapped the woman.

"What? How can you be sure?"

"My dog was dead—I was having it brought home to be buried."

* * *

O'Toole asked the veterinarian in town, "Got anything to cure fleas on a dog?"

"That depends," replied the vet. "What's wrong with them?"

* * *

Mrs. Conlan went into a Rochester department store and said she wanted to knit a sweater for her dog. "What size?" asked the salesgirl.

"Oh, I really don't know," said the woman. "I have him out in the car."

"Okay, suppose you bring him in here so we can measure him," suggested the girl.

"My goodness, I couldn't do that," replied Mrs. Conlan. "This sweater is to be a surprise!"

* * *

Merryman Mark Padow, top dog of the Paint & Coatings Association, makes merry with this madcap cutie:

Beecham bred prize bulldogs. One day he was walking Rocky, his grand champion, down the street, when Foster appeared walking a strange, yellowish animal, the oddest-looking dog Beecham had ever seen.

The animals began to growl at each other, and with a vicious swipe, the yellow one bit the prize bulldog's head off.

"What kind of dog do you call that?" shouted Beecham.

"Well," replied Foster, "before I cut off his tail and painted him yellow, folks called him an alligator."

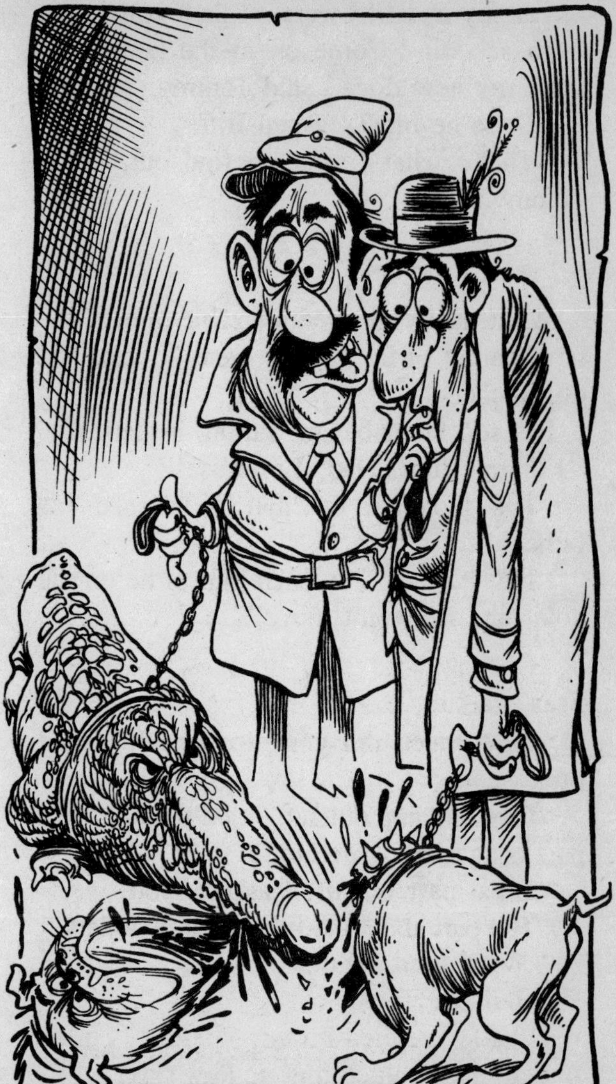

Tommy and Biff were on their way home from school. "Come on in the house and meet my new dog," said Tommy.

"Does he bite?" asked Biff.

"That's what I want to find out," said Tommy.

* * *

When Kelly gnawed a sizable hole in the new carpet, Mr. Fallow went to call the dogcatcher.

His son Peter began wailing hysterically. "I'll train him, Dad. I promise!"

"It's too late for that," snapped his father.

"No, it's not. I'll teach him to lie on the hole, and he won't move!"

* * *

"How much did your dog cost?" asked little Scott.

"Five hundred dollars," said Ryan. "He's part beagle and part bull."

"What part is bull?" asked Scott.

"The part about the five hundred dollars."

* * *

Arnie Shapiro, a Penn State junior, schemed to get money from his dad who was nuts about his Yorkshire terrier, Pinky. Arnie wired his dad: SEND PINKY AND $500. WILL TEACH DOG 100 WORDS.

Shapiro sent the dog and the money. Three weeks later this telegram arrived: PINKY DOING GREAT. FOR ANOTHER $500, HE WILL BECOME THE MOST INTELLECTUAL ANIMAL IN THE WORLD.

Shapiro wired the cash. Soon he had furnished thousands for the canine's education. Now school was over and Shapiro awaited Arnie and his beloved Pinky.

Finally, his son arrived, but without the dog. "Where's Pinky?" asked Shapiro.

"Pop, I've got bad news. I was in the bathroom shaving, Pinky was sitting on the throne reading *Playboy*. Suddenly he said, 'Hey, is your dad still having an affair with the Mexican maid?' I got so mad I took the razor and slit his throat."

"Oh, God!" exclaimed Shapiro. "My dear, darling, little Pinky! My beloved, sweet baby! You killed him?"

"Yes, Pop."

"Are you sure he's dead?"

*   *   *

Did you hear about the two guys who were cycling madly on a tandem bike while a dog was chasing them, trying to throw a bucket of water on them?

*   *   *

Brenda and Ronni were chatting at a cocktail party. "Doesn't it embarrass you to see your husband flirting so shamelessly with all the younger women?" asked Brenda.

"Oh, I just let him have his innocent pleasure," said Ronni. "It's really very harmless. He's like a puppy chasing automobiles. He wouldn't know what to do if he caught one. He just wants to bark at them a little."

* * *

Christine recently got a dog and was proudly demonstrating his good points to her friend Barbi.

"I know he's not what you'd call a pedigreed dog," she said, "but no prowler or stranger can come near the house without his letting us know about it."

"What does he do?" asked Barbi. "Bark the house down?"

"No, he crawls under the sofa."

* * *

Glady's Altshuler, the dynamic Los Angeles office designer, dazzles clients with this dandy:

At 3:00 A.M. Suleiman phoned his Bel Air neighbor and said, "Your dog is disturbing my sleep. He is barking under my bedroom window." He hung up the phone before the sleepy neighbor could answer him.

The following morning at 3:00 A.M. his neighbor phoned him and said, "You know what? I don't have a dog."

* * *

Young Phillip went out on his first business venture: selling magazine subscriptions. Within fifteen minutes he came back waving fifty dollars worth of subscriptions.

"Wonderful! I'm proud of you," said his father. "But how did you sell them so quickly?"

"I sold them all to one man," replied the boy. "His dog bit me."

* * *

Duffy was bitten by a dog and immediately went to his doctor's office.

"Look here," said the M.D., "don't you know my office hours are from 9 to 12 in the morning?"

"You know it and I know it but the dog didn't know it," replied Duffy.

* * *

Fleming's dog, Duke, had died. He had loved him like a son and wanted to have an elaborate burial ceremony. Fleming went to a nearby Baptist church to make the arrangements.

"I'm sorry," said the minister, "but it would be blasphemous to bestow upon a dog the solemn ritual we offer a human being. Try the synagogue two blocks down."

Rabbi Gottesman was even more discouraging. "You must understand," he said, "that a dog is ritually unclean. Try the Catholic church. Maybe they can help you."

Father McNamara listened and shook his head. "I appreciate your feelings, but it cannot be done."

"If it can't be, Father, it can't be," said Fleming. "I was prepared to donate ten thousand dollars to any church that took care of my little Duke."

"One moment, my son," said the priest. "Did I understand you to say that the dog was a Catholic?"

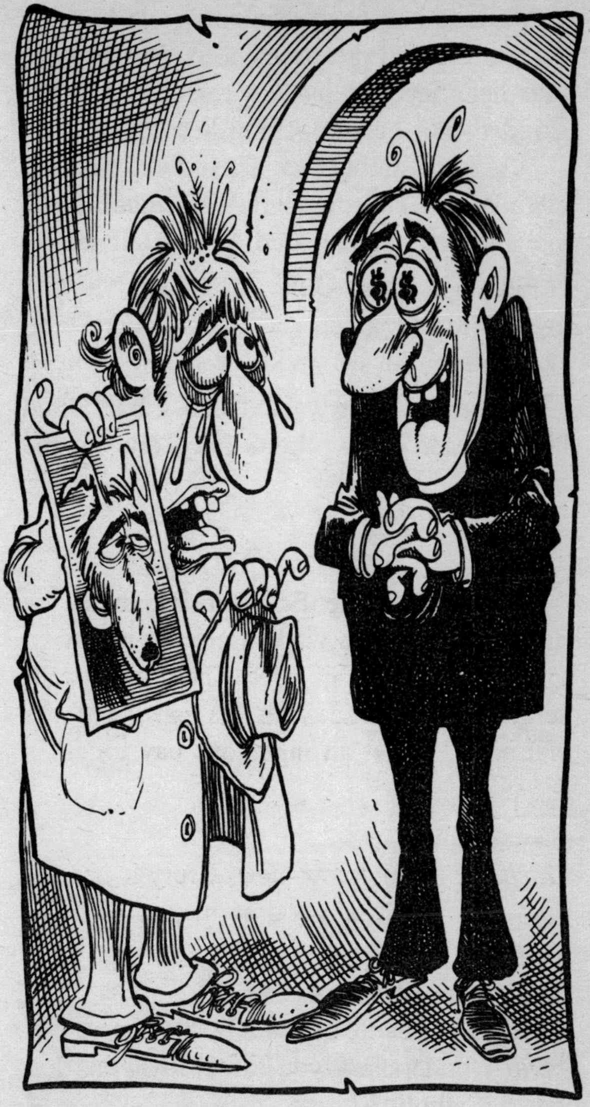

Marlene had been drinking quite heavily. As she crossed the street, a St. Bernard ran into her. Seconds later, a tiny compact car skidded into her, knocking her down.

When the ambulance arrived she told the attendant, "The dog didn't do much damage but the tin can tied to his tail nearly killed me."

* * *

Or the dog that walked into a bar, lifted his leg, and said: "Let's have one on the house."

* * *

Fido spotted the first parking meter he had ever seen. He walked around it slowly, examining it from all sides. Then he stopped, scratched his head with his paw, and exclaimed, "What an ingenious pay toilet!"

* * *

Husband: You know dear Bruty's hearing isn't as good as it used to be.
Wife: Nonsense, come here Bruty. Good dog, now sit!
Husband: There, I told you so.
Wife: All right, I'll clean it up.

* * *

Then there was the dog who saw a sign that said: "Wet Paint"—and he did.

* * *

Happiness is seeing a dog pass your newly planted lawn without stopping.

* * *

Little Quincy pointed to the two dogs and asked what they were doing. "Well," said his father, "the dog in the back has sore front paws and the dog in front is helping him home."

"Just like humans," commented the boy. "Try to help someone and you get screwed every time."

* * *

Why was the dog in court?
He had a barking ticket.

* * *

The sales clerk in a Cincinnati department store noticed Mrs. Falkner carefully examining various displays.

"Are you looking for anything in particular?" asked the clerk.

"I have to get my dog a present or he'll bite my husband again."

* * *

A beggar was plodding along Fifth Avenue with a small dog. Around the dog's neck was a sign:

PITY THE BLIND

Fitzpatrick dropped a quarter into the cup and then cried, "Was that a half dollar I gave you?"

"No," replied the beggar, "it was a quarter."

"So you're not blind then, after all?"

"Hold on," said the beggar. "It's the dog that's blind, not me."

*   *   *

Dave: Is your dog a pointer or a setter?
Ryan: Neither. He's a disappointer and an upsetter.

*   *   *

Elroy's father came home and found a sign in front of the house that read: DOG FOR SALE—FIFTY CENTS. "Fifty cents is too low a price for a dog," he said to the boy. "You've got to think big."

Next morning the sign said: DOG FOR SALE—$10,000.

When Dad got home that night the sign was gone. "Did you sell your ten thousand dollar dog?" he asked.

"Sure did," said Elroy. "I got two five thousand dollar cats for him."

*   *   *

Bruno and Max, two springer spaniels, met on a street corner and got into a conversation.

"I'm waiting for my girl," said Bruno.

"Me, too," replied Max. "Mine's beautiful. A wirehaired terrier."

"That's a coincidence. So's mine."

"And she has the softest fur, and the cutest little red spot over her right eye."

"What do you know about that?" barked Bruno. "Mine has, too!"

"Really?" moaned Max. "Does yours have a white spot on her left cheek and a short-cropped tail?"

"Why . . . yes."

"Say, is her name Duchess?"

"Yeah . . . you don't suppose—"

"Uh-huh! Aren't bitches women!"

*   *   *

Mama flea looked worried. When Papa flea asked why the sadness, she replied, "All our children are going to the dogs."

*   *   *

"How come you love your dog so much?"

"I happen to like my dog's philosophy of life. 'If you can't eat it or screw it, piss on it.' "

* * *

Pennock, a Manhattan bank veep, was about to cross Fifth Avenue when he noticed a funeral procession coming down the street. Two hearses were traveling side by side. Behind them walked a man dressed in black with a huge Doberman pinscher straining on a leash. Behind him walked thirty men in single file.

In awe of the procession, Pennock sidled up beside the man with the dog and asked, "Whose funeral is this?"

"My wife's and mother-in-law's," he replied.

"What happened?"

"This dog killed them."

"Can I borrow it for a week?" asked the bank exec.

"Get to the end of the line!"

About the Author

This is the 44th "Official" joke book by Larry Wilde. With sales of more than ten million copies, it is the biggest selling humor series in publishing history.

Larry Wilde has been making people laugh for over thirty years. As a stand-up comedian, he has performed in top night spots with stars such as Debbie Reynolds, Pat Boone, and Ann-Margret.

His numerous television appearances include *The Tonight Show*, *The Today Show*, *Merv Griffin*, and *The Mary Tyler Moore Show*.

Larry's two books on comedy technique, *The Great Comedians Talk About Comedy* (Citadel) and *How the Great Comedy Writers Create Laughter* (Nelson-Hall), are acknowledged as the definitive works on the subject and are used as college textbooks.

A recognized authority on comedy, Larry is also in constant demand on the lecture circuit. He speaks nationwide to corporations, associations, and healthcare facilities about the benefits of laughter in his keynote speech "When You're Up to Your Eyeballs in Alligators." Larry also conducts executive seminars and humor workshops.

In 1976 Larry Wilde founded National Humor Month. It is celebrated across the

U.S. to point out the valuable contribution laughter makes to the quality of our lives. National Humor Month begins each year on April Fools' Day.

Larry lives on the northern California coast with his author-wife Maryruth.